-- AUG 2018

D1610600

Ina Boyle (1889–1967)
A Composer's Life

Ina Boyle

(1889–1967)

A Composer's Life

With an Essay on the Music by
Séamas de Barra

ITA BEAUSANG

CORK UNIVERSITY PRESS

First published in 2018 by
Cork University Press
Youngline Industrial Estate
Pouladuff Road, Togher
Cork, Ireland

© 2018 Ita Beausang and Séamas de Barra

All rights reserved. No part of this book may be reprinted or reproduced or utilised in any electronic, mechanical or other means, now known or hereafter invented, including photocopying and recording or otherwise, without either the prior written permission of the publishers or a licence permitting restricted copying in Ireland issued by the Irish Copyright Licensing Agency Ltd., 25 Denzille Lane, Dublin 2.

British Library Cataloguing in Publication Data
A CIP record for this book is available from the British Library.

ISBN: 978-1-78205-264-7

Printed in Malta by Gutenberg Press
Print origination & design by Carrigboy Typesetting Services, www.carrigboy.com

www.corkuniversitypress.com

Contents

Preface

When in 2006 I was originally invited to write on the life and works of the Irish composer Ina Boyle (1889–1967) I had heard neither her name nor her music, although she was the first Irishwoman to undertake a symphony, a concerto or a ballet, and was also one of the most prolific composers in twentieth-century Ireland. Great strides have been made in the years since then. Her cause has been taken up, notably by the Ulster Orchestra for the BBC in Belfast, the Callino and RTÉ Contempo string quartets, and the ground-breaking Composing the Island festival at the National Concert Hall in Dublin as part of RTÉ 1916 and Ireland 2016 centenary celebrations. A website has been established – www.inaboyle.org – which provides information on her music internationally. The rising profile of her work fits in with Martin Adams' contention, in his article 'History in the Making' in *The Invisible Art: A Century of Music in Ireland 1916–2016*, that the appearance of monographs on the lives and music of twentieth-century Irish composers over the past thirteen years is indicative of a new kind of cultural confidence about Irish classical music in general.

Ina Boyle's sheltered background in Enniskerry, County Wicklow, seems a most unlikely environment for a composer. Her early musical influences came from a violin-making father and lessons with governesses. There were no opportunities for attending concerts or for hearing orchestral music. It is difficult to imagine what gave her the impetus to become a composer as she studied theory and harmony from an early age with Samuel Myerscough and took correspondence lessons with Charles Wood.

The pattern for her musical life was firmly established when she continued her studies with the English musicians C. H. Kitson and Percy Buck, who had taken posts for short periods in Dublin. She did not pursue a formal course in music study in either of the most obvious Dublin institutions, the Royal Irish Academy of Music or Trinity College Dublin, but opted instead for one-on-one tuition. The selection of her orchestral rhapsody *The Magic Harp* for publication by the Carnegie United Kingdom Trust in 1920 set the seal on her career as a composer. Her next musical destination would add new dimensions to her life and career. On her visits to London for private lessons with Ralph Vaughan Williams she went to concerts and art exhibitions and enjoyed a range of musical activities that were unavailable in the Dublin of the inter-war years. Vaughan Williams was her mentor for sixteen years, until her travels ended with the outbreak of the Second World War.

The aim of this monograph is not only to chronicle Boyle's life and to place her output in context, but also to explain why so little was known about her, why she was forgotten for so many years and why so few of her works have been published or performed. Her friend Elizabeth Maconchy, who gave Boyle generous support during her lifetime and was her musical executor after her death, offered an explanation in her *Appreciation* of the composer:

> But living out of the world, though it suited her temperamentally, had the disadvantage that she made very few musical contacts and that her music remained little known and almost unperformed. All composers need to hear performances of their work, not only for stimulation and encouragement but in order to learn their craft and advance their technique.[1]

She lived all her life out of the world, in the Enniskerry home she loved so much, not far from the Irish capital, Dublin, but somehow a whole universe away. She kept faith with composition through a lifetime that spanned two world wars, the 1916 rebellion, the War of Independence, the Civil War and the economic war; and she was witness to the many social and demographic changes that were taking place in Ireland. She was a dutiful daughter whose strength came from within, through her intellectual interests, her love of nature and her surroundings. Her inspiration came from poetry, literature and the classics, combined with a deep religious faith and an eclectic mix of cultures and languages.

Throughout her life she worked on a constant stream of orchestral, chamber, choral and vocal music, including three symphonies, a violin concerto, ballet music and an opera. Despite rejection, she remained hopeful as she tirelessly circulated her music to publishers and performers, though she did not move in the commercial and social worlds in ways that would have furthered her music. She was reclusive, even other-worldly. Her music was concentrated in the minor mode and did not keep pace with the times or with popular trends. Perhaps her themes were too sombre for a changing world in search of distraction. She never won the recognition that Vaughan Williams hoped for her, yet her commitment to her vision remained intact as she followed her own path as a composer. It is hoped that this opportunity to revisit her life and the ongoing upsurge of interest in her music will help to bring the voice of this long-neglected Irish composer to a wider audience.

ITA BEAUSANG

Acknowledgements

While writing this book, I received generous help and invaluable support from many people. They accompanied me on a ten-year journey to reconstruct the life and music of Ina Boyle and gave me incalculable assistance along the way.

My deepest gratitude is due to the editors, Séamas de Barra and Patrick Zuk, whose vision inspired the publication of this series of monographs on twentieth-century Irish composers. Their scholarship and insight were available to me at all stages of the process. When publication of the book was suspended owing to the discontinuation of the music series by Field Day Publications, the editors approached Cork University Press, where they received a positive response. I am particularly grateful to Mike Collins, Publications Director, the Editorial Committee, and to Maria O'Donovan for her ongoing assistance.

I also wish to express my heartfelt gratitude to the following agencies and individuals whose support and goodwill have contributed to the completion of the book: Boyle and Crampton family members: Adrian Boyle, Tony Boyle, Jane Crampton, Penny Lang, Simon Duckworth, Joan Hutchings, Jean and Patrick Cangley and, in particular, Katie Rowan, who has been a tireless advocate on behalf of Ina Boyle; Michael Dervan for his unfailing encouragement and wise counsel; the Ina Boyle Development Committee: Kenneth Baird, David Byers, Ronald Corp, Ian Fox, Jonathan Grimes, Kerry Houston, Nicola LeFanu, Emma O'Keeffe (curator of www.inaboyle.org), Katie Rowan; Trinity College Dublin: Roy Stanley, Music Librarian, for his expertise in securing copyright agreement, Jane Maxwell, Principal Curator, Estelle Gittins, Aisling Lockhart, Caoimhe Ni Ghormain and Linda Montgomery, who were extremely helpful in allowing me to access scores and documents over the years in TCD Manuscripts and Archives Research Library, Sharon Sutton of Digital Resources and Imaging Services; Síle Ní Thiarnaigh, who catalogued 'Compositions by Ina Boyle', presented to TCD Library by Doreen Boyle in 1967; Contemporary Music Centre: Jonathan Grimes, Niamh Heery, Caitriona Honohan, Susan Brodigan; National Library of Ireland: Tom Desmond, Hanora Faul, Joanna Elizabeth Kirwan, Gerard Lyne, Martin McElroy; Boole Library, University College Cork: Garret Cahill; Fleischmann Library, CIT Cork School of Music: Clare Dwyer; Bournemouth Music Library: Barry Meehan; Library Staff, Dublin City Library and Archive, Pearse Street; Music Library, Henry Street; National

Archives, Bishop Street, Dublin 8; Representative Church Body Library, Churchtown, Dublin 14; Raidió Telefís Éireann: Robert Canning, Lindsay Dowling, Francis Hughes, Brian Lynch, Malachy Moran, Niamh O'Connor, John O'Kane, Brian O'Rourke; BBC Sound Archives: Francis Jones; BBC Northern Ireland: Declan McGovern; Diana Ambache and the trustees of the Ambache Charitable Trust for generous funding; for typesetting and editing manuscripts: David Byers (string quartet and *Still falls the rain*), Sarah M. Burn (violin concerto, the '*Glencree*' symphony, *A Sea Poem* and *Colin Clout*), David Rhodes (*Three Songs by Walter de la Mare*), Roy Holmes ('Eternity' and 'My boy Jack'), Emma O'Keeffe (*Elegy, Psalm, Three Ancient Irish Poems*); CD recordings: Aylish Kerrigan (mezzo-soprano), Dearbhla Collins (piano), Nadège Rochat (cello); David Darcy, Chamber Choir Ireland; Royal Dublin Society: Mary Kelleher and Johanna Suhr; City of Birmingham Symphony Orchestra: Beresford King-Smith; Ralph Vaughan Williams Trust: Hugh Cobbe; Leinster School of Music: Gloria Mulhall and Sheila Murphy; Maritime Museum: David Snook; Stainer & Bell, Banks Music Publications.

I particularly wish to thank the following people who assisted me in many different ways during my journey: John Ashby, Kenneth Baird, Elizabeth Beazley, Edward Bisgood, Bernard Blay, Chris de Burgh, Seóirse Bodley, Margaret Cable, Judy and Lachlan Cameron, Ronald Corp, Claire Cunningham, Sheila Larchet Cuthbert, Diane Davison, Noel Doyle, Anna Dunlop, Mark Fitzgerald, Lewis Foreman, Michael Garton, Gerry Hickey, Una Hunt, Roy Johnston, Sonya Keogh, Máire Larchet, Patricia McCarry, Dean William Morton, Blanaid Murphy, Éimear Ó Broin, Maurice O'Connell, Evin O'Meara, Catherine Porteous, Henry Probert, Canon Bob Reed, Canon Ricky Rountree, Sharon Rubin, Joan Stokes, David Sulkin and Jean-Pierre Surget.

For copyright permission I am indebted to the Ina Boyle Estate and the Board of Trinity College, the University of Dublin; the Ralph Vaughan Williams Charitable Trust; Nicola LeFanu and Antony Bye; letter from Edith Sitwell to Ina Boyle 25 February 1952 by Edith Sitwell reprinted by permission of Peters Fraser & Dunlop on behalf of the Estate of Edith Sitwell; extracts from 'An Old Woman' and 'Invocation' (*Collected Poems Edith Sitwell*, Duckworth Overlook, 2006) reprinted by permission of Peters Fraser & Dunlop on behalf of the Estate of Edith Sitwell.

Finally, my thanks are due to my brother, Dr Edmund Hogan, SMA, for reading the draft and for his meticulous attention to revisions and format, and to my children for their unstinting support and patience.

Abbreviations

BL	British Library
BSO	Bournemouth Symphony Orchestra
CBSO	City of Birmingham Symphony Orchestra
CEMA	Council for the Encouragement of Music and the Arts
CMC	Contemporary Music Centre
CSO	Cork Symphony Orchestra
DOP	Dublin Orchestral Players
EUYO	European Union Youth Orchestra
GPO	General Post Office
ISCM	International Society for Contemporary Music
LPO	London Philharmonic Orchestra
LSO	London Symphony Orchestra
MAI	Music Association of Ireland
MS TCD	Manuscript Library, Trinity College Dublin
NCC	National Chamber Choir
NCH	National Concert Hall
NIRC	New Irish Recording Company
NLI	National Library of Ireland
OUP	Oxford University Press
QHO	Queen's Hall Orchestra
RCM	Royal College of Music
RCSI	Royal College of Surgeons in Ireland
RDS	Royal Dublin Society
RÉ	Radio Éireann
RÉO	Radio Éireann Orchestra
RÉSO	Radio Éireann Symphony Orchestra
RPO	Royal Philharmonic Orchestra
SMEI	Society for Music Education in Ireland
SMI	Society for Musicology in Ireland
TCD	Trinity College Dublin
WAAMA	Writers' Actors' Artists' Musicians' Association
2RN	Irish Radio Station

The Growth of a Composer

Family roots

S elina Adelaide Philippa Boyle was born on 8 March 1889. Three days later a notice in *The Irish Times* announced the birth of a daughter to the wife of Rev. W. F. Boyle MA, Ballyornan, Enniskerry.[1] Selina's mother, Philippa Arabella Boyle, née Jephson (1857–1932), came from a wealthy Protestant family, and the three names given to the baby reflected her distinguished maternal lineage. Her maternal grandmother, Adelaide Jephson, née Crampton (1816–1892), widow of Captain Henry Prittie George Jephson (1813–1866), 87th Royal Irish Fusiliers, lived with her unmarried sister Selina Crampton (1811–1893) at Glenbrook, Enniskerry. They were daughters of the famous Dublin surgeon Sir Philip Crampton, Bart. (1777–1858), who was Surgeon General to the British forces in Ireland and held the title of Surgeon-in-ordinary to George IV and Queen Victoria.[2] Appointed a baronet in 1839 with his seat at Lough Bray, County Wicklow, he was President of both the Royal Zoological Society of Ireland and the Council of the Royal College of Surgeons in Ireland.

There is no mention in the birth notice of Bushey Park, the family house in Enniskerry, which was to be Ina Boyle's much-loved home for the rest of her life. The house had belonged to her intrepid great-uncle, Sir John Fiennes Twisleton Crampton, Bart. KCB (1805–1886), whose colourful diplomatic career spanned forty years across three continents. In 1826 he had entered the diplomatic service as an unpaid attaché in Turin and was transferred to St Petersburg in 1828. He became a paid attaché in Brussels in 1834, moved to Vienna in 1839 and was promoted to secretary of the British legation in Berne in 1844.

A year later he was transferred to Washington DC, where he acted as chargé d'affaires until 1852, when he was appointed Minister Plenipotentiary and

Leabharlanna Poibli Chathair Baile Átha Cliath
Dublin City Public Libraries

Envoy Extraordinary to the United States. During the Crimean War his illegal activity in attempting to recruit American volunteers for service in the British army caused a rupture in diplomatic relations and he was recalled. However, the Prime Minister, Lord Palmerston, appointed him to Hanover in 1857 and he afterwards served as British Ambassador in St Petersburg and Madrid until his retirement in 1869.[3] In 1860 at the age of fifty-four he married the twenty-two-year-old soprano Victoire Balfe, second daughter of the composer Michael Balfe, but three years later the marriage was dissolved.[4] During his travels he had collected valuable paintings, furniture and ornaments which he brought home to Bushey Park, where he died in 1886, three years before Ina was born.[5]

Since he had no children he bequeathed the house and its contents to his two surviving sisters, Selina Crampton and Adelaide Jephson, whose eldest daughter, Philippa Arabella, was to marry the curate of St Patrick's Church, Powerscourt, Rev. William Foster Boyle (1860–1951), a year later. Aged thirty, Philippa was three years older than her husband, and overcame strong family opposition to marrying an impoverished clergyman. Rev. Boyle, who came from Castlecomer, County Kilkenny, had been educated at Trinity College Dublin and was appointed curate at Enniskerry in 1884.

A little over a year after Ina's birth a second daughter, Phyllis Kathleen, was born to the Boyles. Within three more years both Selina Crampton and Adelaide Jephson had died, leaving Bushey Park in the sole ownership of Ina's mother. Selina Crampton had always been close to her brother and had often accompanied him on his travels. She was a talented artist and sketched children, animals and landscapes wherever she went.[6] Sir John was also an accomplished artist, so it is likely that Ina inherited her artistic talent from the Crampton side of the family.[7]

Music lessons

Ina's unusual musical talent, which manifested itself at an early age, came mostly from her father, who was her first teacher. While he was noted for his sermons he was also a skilled cabinet-maker and made violins for a hobby.[8] The sisters were home-schooled and were given violin and cello lessons by their governesses.[9] In 1900, at the age of eleven, Ina took private theory and harmony lessons from Samuel Spencer Myerscough (1854–1940),[10] an English organist, who had come to Dublin in 1899 to teach music at Loreto Abbey, Rathfarnham, and subsequently worked in five other Loreto convent schools in the Dublin area. In 1904 he founded the Leinster School of Music at 43 Harcourt Street; later he examined for the Royal University of Ireland and lectured at St Patrick's Training College, Drumcondra. He was also active as an organist and gave Sacred Concerts on the new organ in St Peter's Church, Phibsborough, in 1910 and 1911 and in the Church of the Holy Redeemer, Bray, for the new organ fund, in 1914. In 1903 he won a prize at the Feis Ceoil for a five-part motet, *Tui sunt coeli*, which was published by Novello.[11]

Myerscough's rigorous approach to teaching was reflected in a magazine interview in which he stated: 'From the earliest stages there must be thinking. In teaching one must take nothing for granted.'[12] For his eager young pupil he was the ideal exponent of the rudiments of music and, judging from his comments in her manuscript books, they had a relaxed teacher–pupil relationship. Between 1903 and 1906, when in her mid-teens, she worked industriously on theory and harmony examination papers, covering modulation, counterpoint, word setting, form, cadences, intervals and Italian musical terms. Ina kept all her old exercises with the teacher's corrections in red ink; sometimes there were personal touches such as 'Pleasant holiday – keep these notes until you have had a rest'.[13]

Myerscough also encouraged her earliest efforts at composition. The question of modulation was raised in the corrections to a violin and piano duet: 'As to when you can modulate, Wagner said "Do not modulate if you can say what you have to say in the tonic key" but then you can say little comparatively in the tonic key!' But a 'horrid anticipation' was noted in her setting of 'The song of the scythe' by Rosamund Marriott Watson, with the comment: 'This melodic outline is effective but in danger of becoming a personal weakness.' There were also rough sketches for a song: 'The wind that blows among the apple trees/ Is as a harp of sorrow in the spring', from the poem 'The harper's song of the seasons' by Eva Gore-Booth,[14] foreshadowing one of Boyle's most important orchestral works, *The Magic Harp* (1919).

From 1904 Ina was also taking harmony and counterpoint lessons by correspondence with a cousin by marriage, Dr Charles Wood (1866–1926). Born in Armagh, he had been awarded scholarships to the Royal College of Music and Cambridge as well as the first fellowship given for music at the latter institution. He was lecturer in harmony and counterpoint there from 1897, and also taught at the Royal College of Music. In 1924 he succeeded Charles Villiers Stanford as professor of music at Cambridge. His wife, Charlotte (whose mother, Adelaide Wills-Sandford, née Jephson, younger sister of Ina's mother, had died at the age of thirty),[15] met Wood in 1894, when she went to study at the Royal College of Music, with piano and singing as her main subjects. After her marriage, Charlotte often visited her Aunt Philippa at Bushey Park, and it is likely that she took a keen interest in her young cousin's musical development.

Described in an obituary as the best teacher of composition in Europe,[16] Wood launched into his tutelage with exercises in species counterpoint and four-part harmony, which he returned with copious corrections in red ink:[17]

> The work is on the whole very good. The harmonization of the melody being the weak point I think you might work the melody again making the changes I suggest in the 3rd and 4th bars ... Also at the end where the 6/4 is wrongly approached. The rule is that the 6/4 must be approached by skip if the chord before it is in an inversion. If you have Macfarren's harmony book you will find the rules put down very clearly on p. 17 (I think). If you haven't got the book I'll write out the rules for you. I enclose more work for next time. Remember the counterpoint is oral so keep the parts within the compass of the voice you are writing for.

With homework from two teachers Ina found it difficult to keep up with the heavy workload. At the end of August 1904, she wrote a plaintive message: 'I am afraid I cannot do so much next time as all my lessons begin next week.' But Wood was determined that the work should be kept up to schedule:

> I am afraid that I have given you more to do than you would have time for. I thought that you would send what you could and go on working the rest as you are doing. Your Ground Bass improved very much as it went on, the imitation and conclusion section being particularly good. I have to go to Leeds on Monday next. Perhaps you can let me have the rest not later than Monday, if not it must keep for a few days as I shall not get back until Wed. night.[18]

There were other challenges ahead for Ina. On the exercise dated 9 March 1905, Wood wrote: 'This is very well put together but the counterpoint is a little clumsy at times. But that will improve with practice. Have you got all the '48 of Bach?' At the end of April he stipulated: 'You ought to do some double counterpoint. If you have not already got it you had better get the book *Double Counterpoint and Canon* by Bridge, Novello's Primers.' The pressure continued into the summer. On 30 June the message read:

> I am going away today and do not return until July 10th. I shall be able to look at the next work on July 11th if you have time to do it by then. I think that some more double counterpoint with added parts is very much wanted. Nothing shows up the faults in double counterpoint so much as when one is required to add parts.

By March 1906 Ina's task was to score a Bach fugue according to a plan sketched out by her teacher. This according to Wood 'will give you more insight into the structure and working of the fugue than merely reading it through'. She soon graduated to writing a movement for string quartet, and by July she was analysing the Adagio from Beethoven's string quartet Op. 18 no. 1, while continuing to copy fugues every week in open score. She also completed sample Junior Grade theory and harmony examination papers for the years 1907–10, although there is no record of her sitting the examinations.

In September 1910, at the age of twenty-one, Ina commenced harmony and counterpoint lessons with Dr Percy Buck (1871–1947),[19] organist, author and composer, who had just been appointed professor of music at Trinity College Dublin, which was then a non-residential position. As director of music at Harrow from 1901–1917 he was a passionate advocate of the value of music education and delivered his first public lecture on the subject when he took up his post in Dublin. Women students had been admitted to Trinity College in 1904, but with many restrictions. Ina did not enrol for a university course and continued to study part-time and to compose. In many ways Percy Buck was a complete contrast to Ina's previous teachers. His textbook *Unfigured Harmony*, which was published by OUP in 1911, encouraged a freer approach to modulation and harmonisation of melodies than the strict doctrines of Myerscough and Wood. Ina received much practical advice and encouragement from Buck for her early compositions, ranging from admonitions regarding slurs and phrase marks to practical hints on vocal range, word setting and choice of keys.[20] Buck resigned from Trinity College in 1920, was appointed professor of music at the University of London in 1925 and was knighted for services to music education in 1935.

Her next teacher, Dr Charles H. Kitson (1874–1944), an Oxford graduate, came to Dublin in 1913 as organist and choirmaster at Christ Church Cathedral. He was appointed professor of music at University College Dublin in 1916, and professor of theory at the Royal Irish Academy of Music in 1918. In 1920 he returned to London and resigned these posts to take the non-residential chair of music at Trinity College Dublin, which he held until 1935. He taught at the Royal College of Music and published a series of textbooks on harmony, counterpoint and fugue. In his obituary in *The Musical Times* he was described as a fine scholar of impeccable taste.[21] Ina took lessons from him from 1913 as she began to concentrate seriously on composition. She had served an intense apprenticeship with four different teachers and was ready to find her own way as a composer.

Early compositions

Boyle kept her early compositions carefully in her collection of manuscripts. Composed between the ages of fourteen and twenty-five, they consist mostly of songs, some with the teacher's corrections in red ink.[22] Since her father and sister were string players, she often added violin or violoncello parts to the piano accompaniments. Her taste in poetry ranged from popular Victorian poets of the time such as Longfellow, Andrew Lang, Alfred Lord Tennyson, St John Lucas, Rosamund Marriott Watson and William Morris, to Irish writers including Douglas Hyde, George Russell (Æ) and Eva Gore-Booth. Her favourite poet at this time was Jean Ingelow, whose *Songs of Seven* provided several texts. Her preoccupation with Eva Gore-Booth's poem 'The harper's song of the seasons' continued, leading her to write a new melody for the words and add a piano accompaniment. Among her early instrumental compositions an *Adagio* for violin, cello and piano was followed by various sketches for string quartet and cello and piano. Her first complete work, *Romance* (1913), for cello and piano, was carefully corrected by Percy Buck. Curiously, she changed the title to *Elegy* when she orchestrated it. Boyle kept a meticulous record of her compositions and their performances in a black notebook labelled 'I. Boyle. Musical Compositions. Memoranda'.[23] The first song listed in the notebook, 'The last invocation', words by Walt Whitman, dates from 1913. That was the year when, at the age of twenty-four, she received her first public acknowledgement as a composer. At Sligo Feis Ceoil, *Elegy* for cello and orchestra was awarded first prize in the composers' competition and the song 'The last invocation' was awarded second prize. She reported in her 'Memoranda' that she had shown the latter to the singer John Coates[24] and to Hamilton Harty,[25] but that they did not perform it.

Boyle's meeting with Hamilton Harty may have taken place in August 1913 at Woodbrook, Bray, the residence of Sir Stanley Cochrane,[26] who had brought over the London Symphony Orchestra, conducted by Harty, for a week-long series of subscription concerts in the converted sports hall. There was a feast of music, including the first performances of Rachmaninoff's piano concerto no. 2, with local soloist Victor Love,[27] and *Don Juan* by Richard Strauss and Debussy's *L'après-midi d'un faune*. An all-Wagner free matinée was held on the Saturday afternoon 'to compensate for some disappointment to subscribers owing to the lateness of the trains'.[28]

A year later 'a lavish train service' was announced for Rachmaninoff's first appearance in Ireland, at Woodbrook, scheduled for 7 February 1914,[29] but he was unable to fulfil the engagement owing to illness, and the concert was postponed.[30] Alfred Cortot played there later in the month and Hamilton Harty and the London Symphony Orchestra returned to give six more concerts in August. The programmes included works by Rossini, Liszt, Wagner, Gluck, Scriabin, Ravel and Tchaikovsky, many of which were certainly unfamiliar to Irish audiences.[31] Although the outbreak of the First World War precluded any further visits to Woodbrook by English orchestras, some concerts by local musicians continued to take place there.

Concerts were also held in the Arcadia Ballroom in Bray. In 1915 Boyle's setting of 'The joy of earth' by George Russell was 'finely rendered' by Madame Nora Borel, a local soprano and singing teacher, at a concert there in aid of the Royal Engineers' Comfort Fund, at which the audience included some wounded soldiers.[32] The war affected the Boyle family directly when Captain Grenville Fortescue, husband of their cousin Adelaide Jephson and father of two children, was killed in action in 1915 at the age of twenty-eight. Another cousin, Lieutenant Patrick Bryan Sandford Wood, RAF, elder son of Charlotte and Charles Wood, aged nineteen, was killed on active service in an aeroplane accident in 1918.

In 1916, Boyle's setting of Rudyard Kipling's poignant poem 'Have you news of my boy Jack?'[33] had resonance for many of her neighbours whose sons and husbands were missing in action. On Easter Sunday 1919 a brass communion rail and chancel, designed by Lord Powerscourt, 'to record the glorious memory of those of our Parish who gave their lives in the Great War', was dedicated at St Patrick's Church, Enniskerry.[34]

Two anthems composed by Boyle in 1915, 'He will swallow up death in victory' and 'Wilt not Thou, O God, go forth with our hosts?'[35] and a choral and orchestral setting of 'Battle hymn of the Republic', reflect her preoccupation with current events. She had arranged to have the first anthem published by Stainer & Bell, as Dr Kitson said he would perform the work at Christ Church Cathedral. She noted in her 'Memoranda' that 'afterwards he said that he did not like it so well on second thoughts so it never was sung'.[36] Boyle's setting for chorus and orchestra of 'Soldiers at peace' (1916), a poem by Captain Herbert Asquith, second son of the British Prime Minister, was destined to have a higher profile. She paid £11.7.0 to have the vocal score published by Novello and in 1918 the first review of her music appeared in *The Musical Times*:

> 'Soldiers at peace' (Novello) is a poem by Herbert Asquith set for chorus and orchestra by I. Boyle. The words have a pathos that is sympathetically reflected in the music. A certain striking 'motif' comes about twenty times in the instrumental part, and in a way binds the beginning to the

end. The vocal part-writing is smooth and singable. The piece is a very suitable one for a choral performance in which the programme should have the war note on its pathetic side. It takes about four or five minutes to perform.[37]

A brief reference to the work in a survey of New Vocal Music in *The Times* was less complimentary: 'There are others who do not know when they are putting their hand upon the ark. I. Boyle has set for chorus Herbert Asquith's "Soldiers at Peace" (Novello) without understanding.'[38]

On 6 February 1920 the first performance of the work, which was dedicated to her mother, was given at Woodbrook by Bray Choral Society, conducted by Thomas H. Weaving.[39] R. Turner Huggard, assistant organist at St Patrick's Cathedral, played the wind parts on the organ, and the strings were played by local amateurs, including her sister Phyllis and their governess, supplemented by a number of local professionals: 'It was very successful, and it was the happiest night of my life. Mother, Father and Phyllis all went. I did not play in it as I wanted to hear it but I played later in the other works at the same concert.'[40]

On the following day, a very favourable review appeared in *The Irish Times*:

> When one reads the noble words of Captain Asquith's sonnet one rather feared the temerity of the young Irish composer, Miss I. Boyle. There was no need. Miss I. Boyle has more than promise. Her handling of the orchestral effects as a background to the chorus was what we have grown to call 'masterly'. The writing is always clever and original, especially the violin parts, used to heighten the suggestion of ideals of youth. To the cello is left the picture-touches – very effectively. The choir entered displaying mobility and oneness of movement and a fine tone-equality throughout, the final line rather wavered, and hardly suggested the poet's or, one would think, Miss Boyle's idea. The work was enthusiastically received, Miss I. Boyle having to come from the body of the hall to acknowledge the ovation. One can easily predict for this talented young Irish girl, the daughter of Rev. W.F. Boyle of Enniskerry, a brilliant future if she develops as one would expect.[41]

The Carnegie Trust

One of the routes by which a 'talented young Irish girl' could progress to a future as a composer was through competitions. In 1918 Boyle had entered her

Phantasy for viola and piano for the Cobbett competition, which had been
established in 1905 by the industrialist and amateur musician W. W. Cobbett
(1847–1937) for a Phantasy or one-movement work.[42] Lionel Tertis, the
celebrated viola player, was the judge that year, but her entry was unsuccessful.
The aim of the Carnegie United Kingdom Trust scheme, funded by the Scottish
philanthropist Andrew Carnegie, was 'to encourage British Composers in the
practice of their art' through publication annually of one to six works chosen
by the trustees. It was a godsend for composers, who would retain copyright
and keep the royalties for their works. The list of composers who benefited
from the scheme is a roll call of many of the key figures of twentieth-century
British music. In 1917 Boyle entered *Soldiers at Peace* for the first competition
of the Trust. There were 136 entries, including works by Stanford and Vaughan
Williams. She was gratified when her entry was commended, and placed on the
list of 'Works of Special Merit' for the information of conductors.[43]

A year later Boyle submitted *A Sea Poem* (1918–1919), a set of orchestral
variations, to the Trust. Although it was not recommended for publication
the judges sent her a note, hoping that she would not be discouraged and
asking to see more of her work.[44] She had another composition, a rhapsody
for orchestra, *The Magic Harp* (1919), ready to send. When she showed it to
Dr Kitson 'he was very doubtful and said he thought it was dull, but to send it
if I liked'.[45] She did so and, despite her teacher's reservations, the rhapsody was
unanimously selected for publication from fifty-two entries by three judges,
composer Granville Bantock (1868–1946), conductor Dan Godfrey (1868–
1939) and music historian Henry Hadow (1859–1937). Her previous teacher,
Dr Buck, sent her 'a most kind letter' when the award was announced.[46] Under
the heading 'New Woman Composer/Carnegie Fund Judges' High Praise', the
Daily Mail reported:

> The trustees of the Carnegie Fund for the publication of new works by
> British composers have this year selected the following six works from
> 52 entries: A Concerto Fantasia for piano and orchestra by Mr E.L.
> Bainton, a Rhapsody for orchestra by Miss Boyle, an Irish composer; an
> Overture for orchestra by Learmont Drysdale, an orchestral suite by Mr
> Ernest Farrar, a quintet for clarinet and strings by Herbert Howells, and a
> Nativity Hymn for baritone solo, chorus, and orchestra by Cyril Scott. Of
> Miss Boyle's composition, the adjudicators say 'An imaginative and poetic
> work full of refined and poetic colour, skilfully orchestrated, and effective
> throughout. We have particular pleasure in commending the work of a
> new composer who gives promise of a distinguished career.'[47]

The Patron's Fund

Further good fortune was in store. The Royal College of Music Patron's Fund was another important outlet for British composers. Endowed in 1903 by Sir (Samuel) Ernest Palmer (1858–1948) of Huntley and Palmer, biscuit manufacturers, it provided funding for a public rehearsal and performance of new music by composers who were under forty years of age and were British subjects. It was not confined to students of the Royal College of Music, so Boyle was eligible to apply. In 1918 she submitted *A Sea Poem* to the Patron's Fund, 'who kept it over two competitions and finally chose *The Magic Harp,* which was there at the same time'.[48]

There was considerable press attention for its first performance on 8 July 1920 by the LSO, conducted by Adrian Boult:

> Through the operation of the Patron's Fund, the public at the rehearsal held yesterday at the Royal College of Music were able to make acquaintance with the work that is being done by the Carnegie Trust. One of the compositions to which the fund has given its grant was included in the day's programme. It is a Rhapsody for orchestra composed by Miss Ina Boyle. The award has been well bestowed. Miss Boyle's music which sets itself to illustrate the Irish legend of the 'Magic Harp' is not only effective but well planned, idiomatic, and authoritative. Miss Boyle writes with decision and charm, a rare combination that gives her music a quality of its own. Her style is thoroughly British in the best sense, for she speaks in her own tongue. It is satisfactory to find a composer of this quality in our midst, as it is equally gratifying to know that the Carnegie Committee is ready to encourage music of this character. There is no question that the work should be heard again.[49]

The reviews that she received from Woolgar & Roberts Press Cutting Agency, and which she preserved carefully, were mostly favourable. *The Pall Mall Gazette* highlighted the Irish connection:

New Irish Composer
First Performance of Picturesque Rhapsody

The last announcement of the Carnegie Trust awards introduced a new name to the musical world, that of an Irish composer, Miss Ina Boyle. Her rhapsody, 'The Magic Harp' named after the legendary Durd Alba of the Celtic countries was included in yesterday's orchestral rehearsal held under the auspices of the Patron's Fund. It is a picturesque, imaginative work, showing skill and promise rather than actual achievement. It is, however, original enough to justify the encouragement the decision of the Trust has given this young composer.[50]

According to *The Daily Telegraph* critic:

It is undoubtedly the work of a very talented young musician but at rehearsal its Wagnerian influence appeared too strong for one to determine its precise value as a creative effort. Of Irish idiom of the conventional kind it is comparatively free. It seems to require a stage – perhaps even a ballet – for its proper appreciation. One is conscious of nothing occult in the spasmodic strains of the harp but further acquaintance with the music may make it sound less earthly.[51]

But a writer in *The Sunday Telegraph* was less impressed:

I must confess to a slight disappointment with Miss Ina Boyle's Rhapsody, 'The Magic Harp' which was rehearsed this week under the auspices of the Patron's Fund. The selection of this work by the Carnegie Trust prepared one for something more striking, but perhaps the award was meant for encouragement. Certainly without training this Irish lady has got very far. The rhapsody has its qualities but individuality is not amongst them.[52]

The review in *The Strad* was somewhat patronising:

Miss Ina Boyle, on the other hand, showed much more real skill and even accomplishment in her Rhapsody 'The Magic Harp'; I should not be surprised to hear that this work has been accepted for public performance somewhere or other. It is worthy of being played again for it is certainly picturesque. Miss Boyle tries for rather too much perhaps, as though she was afraid of saying something too clearly lest it be thought too ordinary or commonplace. This is a common failing with the inexperienced ...[53]

In December 1920, a review of the first public performance of the Rhapsody by the Bournemouth Symphony Orchestra, conducted by Dan Godfrey, who had been one of the Carnegie Trust judges, welcomed 'the advent of another recruit to the small company of women composers and though *The Magic Harp* cannot be accounted a work of great significance or originality it yields no small measure of fragrance and charm'.[54]

Carnegie Collection of British Music

The publication in 1921 of *The Magic Harp* by Stainer & Bell as part of the Carnegie Collection of British Music set the seal on Boyle's previous efforts. At the age of thirty-three she had succeeded in a prestigious competition and had achieved success. As an unknown woman composer from a remote Irish village she could take her place among her peers. Rather ironically, in view of his original doubts about it, she dedicated the work to Dr Kitson, 'as it was the only thing that had had any public recognition'.[55] A new wave of reviews greeted the publication of the works. *Tam O'Shanter*, the concert overture by the late Learmont Drysdale, which was also selected by the Carnegie Trust, actually dating from 1890, gave the critic from *The Daily Telegraph* some ammunition:

> The story of the first is almost ancient history, for it was in the year 1890 that it won a prize of thirty guineas offered by the Glasgow Society of Musicians for the best concert overture ... Miss Boyle's Rhapsody 'The Magic Harp' bears on the flyleaf a quotation from Eva Gore-Booth which runs: 'The Durd Alba (the wind among the apple trees) was the magical harp of the ancient gods of Ireland ...' The modernity of March–November 1919 when the rhapsody was being composed seems to have left Miss Boyle unmoved, and although a fuller orchestra is required than for 'Tam O'Shanter' it, too, might have been written in 1890, to judge from the technique employed. Yet the spirit is independent enough, and as a first orchestral essay – the first, we mean, made public – it is of undoubted value, and again the Carnegie adjudicators have been wise as they have been generous.[56]

A writer in *Musical Opinion* reached the same conclusion:

> Recent additions to the Carnegie Collection of British Music published by the above firm include two orchestral scores and a chamber music work. Neither of the orchestral works can be considered as representative of modern music. One of them is a concert overture, *Tam O'Shanter*, by Learmont Drysdale, which was first performed by Manns at one of the Glasgow Choral Union concerts so far back as 1891; and the other is a rhapsody, 'The Magic Harp' by Ina Boyle which contains some pleasant and attractive music of a not very novel kind.[57]

However, other critics found more appealing qualities in the work. Harvey Grace, editor of *The Musical Times*, considered that it was far better in every way than *Tam O'Shanter*: 'A mere glance at the score shows qualities that make us wish for an opportunity for hearing the work.'[58] Watson Lyle identified some interesting influences:

> The writing here is up-to-date, without being ultra-modern. Both in her use of the harp and the wood-wind the composer recalls certain passages in the symphonic poems 'Phaeton' and 'Le Rouet d'Omphale' of Saint-Saëns. The suggestion of the wind among the apple-tree branches and other Aeolian sounds is charming. The work should be frequently heard and is quite short.[59]

It is noteworthy that Ina Boyle was the only female composer represented in the Carnegie Collection of British Music. Under the headline 'A Musical Discovery', the *Evening Standard* announced:

> Sudden Fame for Irish Woman Composer
>
> The judges appointed by the Carnegie Fund for the publication of new works by British composers have given high praise to a rhapsody for orchestra submitted by Miss I Boyle, an Irish composer, who, they say 'gives promise of a distinguished career'. Miss Boyle who has thus suddenly leaped into fame was hitherto unknown to the London musical public. The Royal College of Music, always on the lookout for new talent, had through its Patron's Fund accepted some of Miss Boyle's work for rehearsal. She was not a student of the Royal College of Music, however. Miss Boyle, who lives at Bushey Park, Ennis Kerry [*sic*], Co. Wicklow, is within easy reach of the large musical coterie in Dublin, where artistic work of a high order is frequently given. Art knows nothing of geographical boundaries, and her future will be watched with interest.[60]

The next performance of the work was in 1923 at a Promenade concert by the Queen's Hall Orchestra, conducted by Sir Henry Wood. The programme included the Symphonic Variations in E minor for piano and orchestra by Bax and Milhaud's second Suite Symphonique. Of the latter work the critic wrote: 'Its trivialities and affectations made no effect whatever, and the listless short-lived applause showed how the listeners' judgement had been whetted by the British work.' After the interval came *The Magic Harp*, which was described as 'a short and not very eventful symphonic poem which says little but says it with perfect sincerity'.[61]

Four years later *The Magic Harp* received a cool reception when it was revived at a BBC Symphony Orchestra concert, in the Queen's Hall, conducted by Sir Landon Ronald:

> An unfamiliar work, 'The Magic Harp' by Ina Boyle was given a hearing. This rhapsody has been published by the Carnegie Trustees and, though what the judges who recommended it say of its poetic quality and delicate colour is true, it raises the question sharply whether the Trustees are spending their money wisely. For it is no more than an ambitious student work. The craftsmanship is good enough and the instrumentation quite suggestive, but the music is short-breathed and there is no extended theme to pull it together. Talent and weakness are often found united in early work but they ought not to appear together in a work bearing a hallmark.[62]

The Daily Telegraph was even more dismissive:

> With one exception the programme of the BBC concert at the Queen's Hall consisted mainly of music which has stood the test of time. The exception was provided by a novelty 'The Magic Harp' by a young Irish lady, Miss Ina Boyle. The work had been highly commended by the judges of the Carnegie Trust. The audience last night was less emphatic in its approval, and truth to tell we found in it little of that 'refined and delicate colour' which made such an impression on the Carnegie judges. It purports to tell the story of a harp that has three strings – 'the iron string of sleep, the bronze string of laughter and the silver string, the sound of which made all men weep'. Perhaps this unusual theme imposed unnatural bounds onto the composer's imagination. It was obviously impossible to aim at anything like the effect of the magic harp. If we had been made to laugh the author would have been accused of flippancy. Had she lulled us to sleep worse things might have been said of her music. Had the men been reduced to tears there might have been a riot if the supply of handkerchiefs had given out.[63]

There was little comfort either for the composer in Ernest Newman's jaundiced piece in *The Sunday Times*:

> Sir Landon Ronald at the BBC concert had hard work to draw any signs of life from the orchestra which was in a particularly sluggish mood. One can make allowances for the BBC in its first season at Queen's Hall

but it really should ask itself before next season whether it is fitting that the wealthiest musical organisation in London should have the poorest orchestra. The novelty of the evening was Ina Boyle's orchestral rhapsody 'The Magic Harp'. This naïve production is published, I understand, by the Carnegie Trust. It would be. The programme note informed us that the Trustees regard the composer as giving 'promise of a distinguished career' and see in the Rhapsody 'an imaginative and poetic work, full of refined and delicate colour.' They would.[64]

The Transfiguration

When Boyle sent the score of an anthem, *The Transfiguration* (1921), for tenor, choir and organ to her former teacher C. H. Kitson, who was living in London, he responded with a letter and five pages of corrections. He warned her against making her work almost impracticable by dividing the trebles into four parts: 'How many choirs can afford this or find four soloists? Your trebles are divided into six parts in page 7 and last page of E flat section. Remember you are not writing for a Chorus (200 voices) but a Cathedral Choir in which trebles vary from 12–20.'[65]

For the organ writing he recommended pieces by Walford Davies, Charles Macpherson, or Bairstow: 'These will teach you more than fifty lessons bearing in mind what I told you.'[66] Having revised the work, Boyle paid £25 to have it published by Novello & Co. She dedicated it to Rev. Canon Henry Kingsmill Moore, canon of St Patrick's Cathedral, who had selected the text. The anthem was performed at a Sunday morning service, on 26 November 1922, in St Patrick's Cathedral by the cathedral choir, conducted by George Hewson.

The Irish Times previewed the occasion with an extensive article entitled 'A New Irish Composer'. It gave information on Boyle's family, and noted that her musical studies had been conducted wholly in Ireland: 'There is something which stirs the imagination in the thought that this lady, who has only left her teens a short time behind, has worked steadily and so undauntedly, without any immediate prospect of hearing a performance of her music.'[67] The writer underestimated the composer's age – she was actually thirty-three years of age.

The performance exceeded all expectations:

> Miss Ina Boyle's anthem entitled 'The Transfiguration', of which so much has been heard, was sung during the morning Service at St. Patrick's Cathedral yesterday, when a large congregation had an opportunity of judging the merits of this new work. In England, Miss Boyle's

compositions have been performed by first class orchestras, and her reputation has already been established in London, but until yesterday none of her work had been heard in Dublin. Dr Hewson, organist of the Cathedral, undertook the anthem, which is very difficult to sing, and demands earnest rehearsal for an intelligent interpretation. That that demand had been fully met was evident by the treatment by the choir yesterday. It was admirably sung, and the organ accompaniment was most effective. Dr Hewson and the choir entered into the spirit of the work and their sympathetic co-operation achieved the best results. The anthem opens with diatonic passages on the organ and a tenor solo. The solo was sung by Mr John Gill who presented impressively the beauty of the words. At the words, 'The fashion of the countenance was altered,' chromatic harmonies were frequently used, and the chorus entered with the words 'and behold Moses and Elias appeared in glory'. The chorus was exceedingly well done, and the music at this point, being very original in design, produced surprising effects. The second part of the anthem, beginning 'Praise the Lord, O my soul', contains many brilliant and effective passages, and harmonically it is the most diatonic. A magnificent climax was reached at a point where the choir divides into first and second chorus for about eight bars. This portion was a vocal masterpiece, and brought the anthem to a brilliant conclusion.[68]

2

Lessons in London

Ralph Vaughan Williams

Boyle was now at a turning-point in her career. She had gained some recognition at home and abroad but she needed another teacher. At the end of 1922 she wrote to Ralph Vaughan Williams requesting composition lessons from him when she next visited London. Vaughan Williams had a strong commitment to teaching and had been appointed part-time professor of composition in the Royal College of Music in 1920. There is no record of what prompted her to approach him, but the fact that two of her previous teachers, Percy Buck and C. H. Kitson, were both teaching in the Royal College of Music at the time may have had something to do with it. It is also possible that Vaughan Williams knew of her through the Carnegie Trust, which had selected his work, *A London Symphony*, for publication in 1917. By February a suitable date was arranged and the lessons began, at the rate of £1 per hour, at the Vaughan Williams home, 13 Cheyne Walk, Chelsea.

Travelling from Enniskerry to London by road, sea and train was a day's journey. For the steamship crossing from Dún Laoghaire to Holyhead and the train journey to Euston she wore galoshes and a herdsman's jacket, and kept her money safely in the pockets.[1] Her first London accommodation was a service flat at 45 Inverness Terrace, Hyde Park, and later she stayed in College Hall, Malet Street, a hostel connected to the University of London. She preserved a total of thirty-two handwritten notes and postcards (including four from Adeline Vaughan Williams) in a folder labelled 'Letters from my beloved teacher Dr Ralph Vaughan Williams O.M., from 1923[2] to 1958, with one from Mrs Ursula V.W. after his death'.[3] Beginning formally, 'Dear Miss Boyle', the letters were mostly concerned with arrangements for lessons. Boyle kept her own record of the lessons from 1928 to 1939, which she carefully copied into a notebook in 1956 as 'A few notes on Lessons from Dr Vaughan Williams'.[4]

From the beginning the lessons did not have a formal pedagogical pattern, but were based on the compositions that she was working on at the time. The works that she brought to the first lesson on 3 February 1923 included her Pastoral for orchestra, *Colin Clout*, which dated from 1921. It had been accepted by the Patron's Fund, and was rehearsed and performed at the Royal College of Music on 22 June 1922 by the (New) Queen's Hall Orchestra, conducted by Adrian Boult. According to her own account *Colin Clout* was 'unsatisfactory', and the press cuttings that she received from Woolgar & Roberts Press Cutting Agency offered some contradictory opinions. Under the rather unwieldy heading, 'Works of Achievement and Promise and Good Construction', she received one favourable mention: 'Ina Boyle made the best show with "Colin Clout", a Pastoral after Spenser's "Shephearde's Calendar" for small orchestra, in which the solo flute had an important part. Both in melodies and treatment it was excellent.'[5]

According to *The Strad*, 'A somewhat lengthy pastoral by Miss Ina Boyle was not badly made but seemed lacking in imaginative qualities.'[6] But even though another writer commented on her 'decided imagination',[7] there was not much encouragement for the composer in *The Times*: 'Miss Ina Boyle's Pastoral "Colin Clout" we thought frankly to be dull and unimaginative and not nearly so assured in technique.'[8] She had already sent the work to Henry Wood but he had turned it down. Undaunted, she sent it to Dan Godfrey at Bournemouth, 'who did not like it but offered to do it at a small concert (not the symphony concerts)'.[9] She did not accept his offer as she did not want to have an 'unsatisfactory work' performed, but to her surprise Vaughan Williams seemed to like it. He suggested strengthening the orchestration and adding several pages, chiefly to improve the climax. When she was in London again in the autumn she showed him the revised version, 'which he said he liked'.[10]

Lessons were also conducted by correspondence. When she sent him 'Two Christmas Songs' (1923) he liked the first one, 'So blyssed be the tyme', very much, but was not sure about the second, 'Tyrle tyrlow', and sent back pencilled corrections. Although she does not mention them in her notes, it is likely that he looked at her settings of Walter de la Mare's 'A song of shadows' and 'A song of enchantment', composed in 1922. There are some pencilled corrections on the manuscripts, and the changes were made when they were published by Stainer & Bell. She also sent him some of her *Gaelic Hymns* (1923–24), to which he responded: 'The settings of the Irish words are quite something *sui generis* and I like most of them very much.'[11]

In her notes Boyle records seven lessons that she had with Vaughan Williams in February 1928, although it was a busy time for him, and his wife Adeline's health was a cause for concern. At the first lesson, on 3 February, he worked on the *Phantasy* for violin and chamber orchestra (1926). When Boyle asked him about the balance between solo and orchestra he said it was hard to judge, as so much depended on the soloist and the number of strings, but 'on the whole he advised keeping the accompaniment very much in the background as it was so annoying to see the player playing and have to strain to hear'. He suggested only a few alterations to the work and said otherwise it was 'quite nice'. He advised her to have some lessons in orchestration from his colleague at the Royal College of Music, Gordon Jacob, 'as he had a special gift for it', but she was unable to do so.[12] He also looked at the song 'When Mary thro' the garden went' (1927), which Boyle had written for her mother's birthday, and said it might be difficult to play the accompaniment really legato and told her to get a good pianist to play it.

Vaughan Williams mentioned that he had read her recent article in *The Dominant* and that he liked the Clandillons' book and asked about the authors, and how they sang. *The Dominant* was a monthly music magazine edited by Edwin Evans and published by OUP from 1927 to 1929. The article in question was her review of *Londubh an Chairn, Songs of the Irish Gael* (Oxford: OUP, 1927), edited by Séamus Clandillon, Director of 2RN, the Irish radio station, and his wife, Margaret Hannagan (Máighréad Ní Annagáin). The review had just appeared in the February 1928 issue.[13] The book, which was published for the Carnegie United Kingdom Trust by OUP, contained a collection of seventy-five songs, most of which, according to the Preface, had been handed down traditionally in the family of Máighréad Ní Annagáin.

A scathing review of the book, by Donal J. O'Sullivan, had appeared the previous November in *The Irish Statesman*,[14] a weekly magazine published in Dublin, edited by George Russell. This led to a series of recriminatory letters in the magazine from both parties,[15] and a libel case a year later. The jury was unable to agree on a verdict, but the defence costs of £2,500 resulted in the demise of *The Irish Statesman*. It is not known whether Boyle was aware of the controversy when she wrote her review, but it is likely that she was well-disposed to a publication sponsored by the Carnegie United Kingdom Trust. She suggested that since the tune of 'Ned of the hill' was not the traditional air but a version composed by Mrs Clandillon in 1901, the original tune should also be included. She showed her familiarity with the genre by mentioning that one of the airs, 'The blackbird and the thrush', had been arranged by Charles Wood, with words by Alfred Percival Graves, and referred to fine translations of Irish traditional religious poems by Dr Alexander Carmichael, Miss Eleanor Hull and Professor Kuno Meyer.

At the next lesson, on 4 February, Vaughan Williams looked at her Rhapsody for soprano and string quartet, 'A dream in May morning' (1927), with text by Chaucer. She had already sent it to the ISCM Festival committee, but it had not been accepted.[16] While Vaughan Williams 'really liked it', he said that 'some of the vocal phrases were too much formed from arpeggios, in an instrumental style', which 'he disliked in some of Weber's melodies – that it was never met with in Palestrina'. He praised her settings of 'A mountain woman asks for quiet that her child may sleep' by P. H. Pearse (1927), and George Herbert's 'Longing' (1925), but he did not like 'The stolen child'. He said it would be better to keep the tune the same in the first two verses, and that it 'over-sophisticated' songs of a simple type to alter the tune in little ways in different verses. He thought that Stanford had done this too much.

Boyle's most ambitious work to date, the '*Glencree*' symphony (1924), had started out as a suite. Vaughan Williams advised her to send two completed movements to the Patron's Fund, and they offered to play them. She asked for a performance of the slow opening movement only, and on 4 December 1925 the *Adagio* was rehearsed and performed at the Royal College of Music by the LSO, conducted by Adrian Boult, who said he thought it was effective.[17] Afterwards Vaughan Williams had commented that it 'sounded well but wanted pulling together'. Boyle had always wanted it to be a symphony, so in 1927 she added a first movement, *Molto moderato*. A year later when she took the score to a lesson on 9 February, Vaughan Williams said that it was 'too scrappy', and that the development especially needed to be longer and more continuous. He added 'if people would only remember that what is wanted is not that they should take each theme and do something with it, but to make a continuous section, using perhaps only a phrase of one or two of the themes, which shall lead on and on till it comes back to the recapitulation'. He thought that she had shortened the recapitulation too much and that is sounded 'as if it had been drastically cut down', and 'it is better to be too long than to be scrappy – you must not be afraid of "doing nothing", that is very important too'.

The next lesson on 11 February was devoted to vocal music. When Boyle showed him Purcell's 'With sick and famished eyes', which she had copied in the British Museum – she had previously used the text for her song 'Longing' – his comment was 'that is rather a wonderful song', and he liked her setting too. He still found 'The stolen child' unsatisfactory, but said that there was no use trying to alter it, and the same applied to 'They went forth'. Of the other songs, 'Blow, blow, thou winter wind' was 'rather a dismal setting of the words but otherwise all right', and he liked the little lullaby 'A mountain woman asks for quiet'. He queried starting the voice and piano together in the former song, as the singer would need to pitch the first note, but, when Boyle said she wanted that, he responded 'then the pianist must only "dab" a note as best he can'. It is clear that their relationship had become less formal as they discussed new works by Janáček and Holst as well as a concert by Elisabeth Schumann that she had attended.[18]

During the following week Boyle worked on the revisions of the orchestral works, and brought the amended short score of the first movement of the symphony to her lesson on 20 February. Vaughan Williams 'thought it improved, but I do not think he liked it at any time, and I quite feel myself that it is not good enough for a symphony'. However, when she asked whether it would be better to abandon it he encouraged her to continue. He had changed his mind about some of the suggestions he had made about the *Phantasy* for violin and orchestra and gave her new instructions. Again they discussed recent concerts; Vaughan Williams confessed that he could make nothing of Schoenberg's third Quartet but that he had enjoyed Purcell's *King Arthur*. When she asked about publishing her songs he advised her to send them again to Stainer & Bell. He also said that he would try to think of a suitable singer for the Chaucer Rhapsody.

At the end of the report of her next lesson, which took place on the following day, Boyle noted: 'This was a very pleasant and kind lesson.' She had brought her *Psalm* for cello and orchestra (1927), which Vaughan Williams seemed to read with interest.[19] At first he said, 'This is a curious work. I think the movements are too short and that it would sound scrappy.' But later he said, 'I daresay it would be effective.' Of the 6/8 section his comment was, 'It is rather dry but I like it', and of the agitated middle section, 'you must be careful not to make a conventionally dramatic start'.

He asked whether she had anyone to play with or whether she had brought her cello to London. He then suggested Joan Elwes as a soloist for the Rhapsody, as 'she sometimes gives adventurous concerts',[20] and gave her his ticket for the Bach Cantata Club concert that evening as he could not use it. As she had shown him all her work she did not expect to have another lesson, but he said that he would be in on Friday 24 February and that she could telephone him if she wanted to come again. So she worked hard on the revisions of the two orchestral works, hired a cello from W. E. Hill, 140 New Bond Street, and telephoned for a lesson. Unfortunately her ability to play the cello was limited. When she tried to play the solo part of *Psalm*, with Vaughan Williams at the piano, she was so nervous that she could hardly play a note:

everything was out of tune and time – it was a perfect nightmare. I think Dr VW was aghast, but he was gentle and patient beyond words and did everything to make it easy for me. He never said a word about its being out of tune, though it must have been agonizing. He only said 'you are not always playing what you have written' and 'I think from always being alone you have got into the habit of shortening long notes. You ought to play with a metronome sometimes and test the things you write by it to see whether you have written what you really want.' He then went over it again 'bit by bit' altering anything that seemed necessary. At the end he said 'It does hang together better than I thought, I daresay it would be effective if well played.'

Boyle 'felt so dreadfully sorry to have gone so utterly to pieces … yet in a way it was one of the most helpful lessons I ever had, and I never felt more grateful to anyone than I did for the consideration and sympathy he showed about it'.

The White Gates

By 1929 Vaughan Williams had moved from his London home of twenty-five years to the Surrey hills he had known and loved since his early childhood. On 15 March 1930 Boyle travelled by train from Waterloo to the White Gates on the outskirts of Dorking. Vaughan Williams had assured her that it was only an hour from London and gave her a sketch map and full directions to the house. The lessons in Dorking marked a more relaxed phase in the teacher/pupil relationship. There were no restrictions on time, 'we could have the whole morning and my wife hopes you will lunch with us and we could go on in the afternoon if necessary'.

Vaughan Williams looked through the first movement of her second symphony, *The Dream of the Rood* (1929–30), and then went through it a second time for the orchestration, suggesting various changes to improve the balance. 'Both he and Mrs Vaughan Williams were kindness itself, and I had a most delightful day, working all the time both all the morning and again after luncheon.' When she showed him a letter of recommendation that Charles Kennedy Scott had sent her about the *Gaelic Hymns*, he advised her to send it to Stainer & Bell and, if it were possible to have them published, to get them to negotiate the price of the words, which he thought very high.

He mentioned that he had heard Arnold Bax's third symphony the night before, and thought it magnificent. There were two more lessons in Dorking on 20 and 27 March, during which Vaughan Williams looked at the rest of the first movement of the second symphony, checking the alterations. He said that 'on the whole he liked it'. He also examined the other movements in detail and suggested improvements. In general he considered that the work was now fit for performance and advised her to show it to Colonel Brase.[21]

In a postscript to a later note he added 'I hope Dublin will do your symphony', but she was destined to suffer disappointment in her efforts to have the work performed. When she sent the work to Adrian Boult he returned it saying that two of the BBC's readers thought it unsuitable and that he 'regretted that he concurred with their decision', and that Henry Wood also had turned it down. In Dublin she got no answer from Brase for three months, so she sent the score to a visiting Swiss conductor, Ernest Ansermet, who returned it without any comment. When she sent it again to Brase he was ill, and it was returned unread. Later she sent the symphony to Professor Donald Tovey, who wrote her an 'interesting letter'.[22]

However, there was some encouragement to be gained from another quarter. At tea in Dorking, Vaughan Williams asked her whether she had ever written any hymn tunes. He was seeking hymns for a supplement to *Songs of Praise*. She was able to supply him with a copy of her setting of Christina Rossetti's hymn for Saint Michael and the All Saints, 'Service and strength' (1929). This was accepted by the hymnal committee, with one slight alteration, and published in 1930 by OUP in the revised edition of *Songs of Praise*.

He looked at her sketch of 'The Land' (Vita Sackville West), but said that he only liked the Prelude and the first 'Winter' movement. Boyle felt that he did not think it was worth continuing, which was also her own opinion. In her 'Memoranda' she noted, 'Sketched several movements but did not complete the work as Betty LeFanu had written a suite on the same subject'.[23] She told him about her unsuccessful efforts to have her *Gaelic Hymns* published, and he suggested Chesters if she was paying for them.

Boyle's role was now fully established as a friend as well as a pupil. On her return to Enniskerry she sent a present of violets by post to Dorking, for which Adeline Vaughan Williams sent a warm note of thanks, ending with the words, 'It was a real pleasure to see you here.'[24] On 10 March 1931, Vaughan Williams arranged her lesson at 30 Glebe Place, Chelsea, as he was in London on that day. He looked at sketches of the ballet the *Virgilian Suite* (1930–31) and *Five Sacred Folksongs of Sicily* (1930). He said 'the sketches of the first three movements of the Suite were promising. He made no suggestions for the first movement, but said the middle section of the *Elegy* needed lengthening a little. He told me to get as much variety as possible in scoring the fugue, as it might be difficult to dance to on account of being more or less the same all through.'

When she told him that she found it hard to judge how much music to allow for the action he said 'that was the great difficulty with ballet and that only experience could help, as so much depended on the size of the stage and similar things. On the whole the tendency was to allow too much music rather than too little.'

Boyle reported with satisfaction that Vaughan Williams 'seemed to like the Sicilian Songs and said it was a very good lot of work I had brought this time'. He enquired whether there was any chance that she could 'go abroad for a little to study', but she said that it was impossible on account of her family commitments. However, she said that she hoped to go to Oxford in July for the ISCM Festival.[25]

Gaelic Hymns

Following the publication of five *Gaelic Hymns* in 1930, a review in *The Musical Times* noted 'they are skilfully written and should sound well: The last two call for much pianissimo singing. All are for unaccompanied voices, and need a good choir.'[26] The gender of the composer, 'I. Boyle', was confused in the notice in *Musical Opinion*:

> The words of the five hymns are translated from the original Gaelic, and a high poetic beauty marks each one of them. The composer in his settings has admirably caught their wayward emotional temperament and writes, often in six real parts, with masterly ease. Three numbers are for chorus and solo voice. 'The Soul Leading' and 'Soul Peace' for SATB and alto solo; 'The Guardian Angel' for TTBB and alto solo; 'Jesu, Thou Son of Mary' opens with delightful responsive work between the three upper and three lower voices. The 'Light'ner of the Stars' is a fine sweeping movement of six-part polyphony.[27]

In March 1931, while Boyle was in London, four *Gaelic Hymns* were sung at a concert in the Aeolian Hall by the Oriana Madrigal Society, conducted by Charles Kennedy Scott. When she spoke to Vaughan Williams at her lesson on the same day about hearing them at rehearsal, he reassured her that things always sounded different at the actual performance. Afterwards she reported that he thought they had sounded even better than he had expected. After she returned home he wrote: 'I'm so sorry I didn't write before. I thought that your motets were splendid and very well sung – it is a pity that the programme led people to think that the *music* as well as the words were traditional.'[28]

According to the critic from *The Times*:

> Ina Boyle's settings of four 'Gaelic Hymns' are new, and are thoughtfully
> written pieces which make skilful use of varieties of vocal colour, such
> as antiphonal singing by men and women, or the contrast of a contralto
> solo with the men's voices. They have the disadvantage common to all
> such arrangements that the harmonic texture sophisticates the original
> feeling of the songs. That is inevitable and moreover the very insistence
> on variety is apt to defeat its own purpose. The four hymns together left
> an impression of monotony, but each one in itself is a piece of tenderly
> reflected music, and all were very sympathetically sung.[29]

Lessons: 1933–39

After Boyle's mother's death on 9 April 1932, Boyle did not visit London again
until the end of May 1933, when the Oriana Madrigal Society included some
Gaelic Hymns on the programme of their summer concert in the Aeolian
Hall.[30] When she enquired from Vaughan Williams about a lesson he answered
that he would be delighted to see her and her work. In the second half of June
she had three lessons at College Hall, at which they made up for lost time
with three choral works: 'Holy art Thou', 'Jesu, that dear boughtest me', and
A Spanish Pastoral (1931); three hymns: 'Leave me O love', 'If God build not
the house', 'He that hath eternal being' (1930); and two orchestral works: *Elegy*
for chorus and orchestra and Concerto for violin and orchestra (1932).[31] At the
first lesson on 17 June, Vaughan Williams said he liked *A Spanish Pastoral* and
did not suggest any changes to it. He thought 'Jesu that dear boughtest me'
too uneventful: 'it just goes on very well from bar to bar but nothing much
happens', and after he had tried it said 'it might sound beautiful if very well
sung, but if not well sung it would be monotonous'. He did not think that the
hymns were suited to congregational unison singing, but said that they would
make good motets.

There was also time for conversation as they discussed a performance the
night before of *Hugh the Drover* at the Royal College of Music. Vaughan
Williams said that he was 'quite converted to Beecham as a conductor, and
he had done wonders with the orchestra, only he thought that he had taken
parts rather too fast, so that they could not get the words in'. He said that
Beecham 'had only looked at the score for the first time about a week before
the performance, and that he had worked the performers terribly hard, but got
a wonderful performance'.

When asked whether there was any truth in the rumour that the *Virgilian Suite* was being performed by the Camargo Society, Boyle replied that she had not heard anything definite. Vaughan Williams advised her to telephone the secretary and ask for an interview about it. He reassured her by recalling his own experiences as a young composer:

> I always tell you young people that you must keep sending your things to people even if they are sent back again and again, as how can they know about them unless you do. When Holst and I were young we sent works to Wood for about ten years and he always sent them back, till at last one year he did one of mine and one of Holst's.

He promised to write her an introduction to Hubert Foss, music editor at OUP, for which she was very grateful. At the next lesson, on 20 June, Vaughan Williams looked at the revisions she had made in the hymns and went through the *Elegy* very thoroughly. He changed the last bar of the vocal part and suggested improvements in the orchestration. In typically self-deprecatory style, Boyle recorded that he 'seemed to like Elegy better than I expected, as I was disappointed in it myself'. He also reminded her to send two of the hymns to OUP.

They worked on the violin concerto at the third lesson on 25 June, and Vaughan Williams 'seemed to like it better' than when he had first looked at it. Since the movements were so short he suggested it would be better to have them leading into one another without a break. He commented that she had carried bareness of harmony to its limit. He also made various suggestions about the scoring. She had good news of an appointment to see Edwin Evans of the Camargo Society about the ballet and mentioned that Anne Macnaghten also wanted to see the score, but Vaughan Williams advised her to leave it with Evans if there was a chance of having the work performed. Unfortunately, there were no further lessons that summer because Vaughan Williams had a fall and was out of commission for at least three weeks. He wrote to apologise, and expressed the hope that something would come of her interview with Edwin Evans.[32]

Following Vaughan Williams' advice, Boyle sent the *Gaelic Hymns* to the ISCM Festival committee, but they were not accepted. Later she sent them to Leslie Woodgate, BBC Chorus Master, who told her that they were already in the BBC reference library. She did not receive much encouragement either from Herbert Sumsion, to whom she sent the hymns for the Three Choirs Festival at Gloucester. He kept the copies but said that he might not use them.

On 27 February 1934, Boyle visited Vaughan Williams in Dorking, bringing the overture for orchestra which she intended to enter in the *Daily Telegraph* competition.[33] He thought that it was good, and made a few suggestions about the scoring. A month later he sent her a note, signed 'Yours very sincerely', wishing her a speedy recovery after her operation. The surgeon for her thyroid operation at St Bartholomew's Hospital in London was Sir Geoffrey Keynes FRCS,[34] younger brother of John Maynard Keynes. During her convalescence she received a very friendly letter from Adeline Vaughan Williams:

> Dear Miss Boyle
>
> Your violets are heavenly. They came at tea-time the day they were sent and the postman could scarcely bear to give them up. Thank you from us all. I was relieved to hear that you were released from the nursing home ... and I do hope that your sister is much better again.[35] We are so sorry for the bad time you have been having.[36]

By November she had recovered and was back in London for a short visit. There was only one lesson at College Hall, at which they concentrated on a new work, the string quartet in E minor. Boyle's report was succinct:

> Dr V.W. liked the material of the first movement but thought the construction unsatisfactory. He made various suggestions which I will try to adopt later. The 2nd movement he thought better constructed, but did not like the material. The last was unfinished, but he said it was quite clear and would probably be all right.

On her return to Enniskerry she received a letter from her teacher: 'Thank you for your letter and cheque. I am so glad you had such a successful time in London. I shall hope to hear the quartet played through in April.' A year later she sent the score to the ISCM Festival committee, but it was not accepted.

On 26 April 1935, Boyle's violin concerto was rehearsed by the BBC Symphony Orchestra, conducted by Aylmer Buesst, with André Mangeot as soloist, but the work was not broadcast. This was a bitter disappointment for her as she had already sent the score to Adrian Boult, who advised her to send it to the BBC. She had also submitted it to the ISCM Festival committee, and sent it to several violinists. Vaughan Williams had expressed an interest in attending the performance, as he was coming to London for a rehearsal on the same day, and asked for details of the time and place. He also gave her the names of three good copyists whom she might find useful.

At the end of the year there was some encouragement for her when one of her earlier works, finally published by Stainer & Bell, was reviewed in *The Musical Times*:

> Ina Boyle, remembered as a Carnegie Trust publication scheme winner, has set 'A Spanish Pastoral', words by the 16th century St. Teresa, for soprano solo (or boys' choir and TBB). The music graciously and with an individual touch paints the scene of the annunciation to the shepherds. This is worth noting for Christmas as well as other use.[37]

At the age of sixty-three, Vaughan Williams, having declined a knighthood some years earlier, accepted the appointment to the Order of Merit. Boyle sent him a congratulatory telegram which he acknowledged. On 25 May 1936, she visited Dorking, where she had 'a most delightful day'. For the past year she had been working on a masque or ballet, *The Dance of Death*, based on Holbein's medieval masterpiece. Vaughan Williams thought that the variations were too short for dancing but that they could be used for concert performance, and suggested the BBC if Sadlers Wells would not do it. He particularly liked the opening fugue, the 'Astrologer', and the 'Duchess variations'. They agreed that the climax of the fugue was inadequately scored and spent most of the time trying to improve it, going back to work on it after tea.

Vaughan Williams made arrangements to look at the second half of the ballet a week later at College Hall, on his way back from a rehearsal for the premiere of his new work, *5 Tudor Portraits*, at Norwich Festival. In a note that she received on her return to Enniskerry he mentioned that he had contacted Frederick May, Musical Director of the Abbey Theatre, Dublin, to get in touch with her, and 'hoped that she did not mind'.

During the next lesson at College Hall on 30 May, Vaughan Williams looked at the rest of the ballet. He said that he wished he could hear it played by Maconchy, and 'to let him know if she was up in town and could do it. He again said he did not see why it should not be played without dancing.' He also wished that the *Gaelic Hymns* could be performed again, as he had liked them so much when he had first heard them. As that was five years ago, Boyle was very pleased that he had remembered them. Perhaps that encouraged her to proceed with another choral work, *Seven Psalms*, a setting of sixteenth- and seventeenth-century texts of the Psalms of David, which she brought to her next lesson at Dorking in April 1937. It was after this visit that Vaughan Williams wrote: 'Many thanks for your letter and cheque. I think it is most courageous of you to go on with so little recognition. The only thing to say is that it sometimes *does* come finally.'[38]

It was the last record of their lessons in England. Although Boyle travelled to London twice in 1938 she did not visit Dorking. In June 1939, Vaughan Williams came to Dublin to receive yet another honorary degree, a D.Mus. from the University of Dublin. He visited her at her home in Enniskerry, where she had what proved to be her final lesson with him. She showed him two new works, *Thinke then, my soule*, a setting from John Donne's 'The Second Anniversarie' for tenor solo and string quartet, and *The Vision of Er*, a mimed drama with music, based on Book X of Plato's *The Republic*.

Meanwhile, when she had done all the corrections, Boyle made numerous efforts to have *The Dance of Death* performed as a ballet in London. She first sent the score to Constant Lambert of the Vic-Wells Ballet and next to the dancer Anton Dolin, who returned it without comment. The BBC returned it with regrets and it was rejected by the Patron's Fund. In 1938 she asked the pianist Charles Lynch to show the work to Mme Marie Rambert, who said it was unsuitable for the Mercury Theatre. He then asked Ninette de Valois of the Vic-Wells Ballet to look at it, but before she had time, war had been declared, and Boyle got the score back without knowing whether or not de Valois had seen it.

Local recognition: 1929–1938

Orchestral concerts in Dublin had been spasmodic since the visits of the LSO to Woodbrook in 1914 but, contrary to popular perception, there was a certain amount of activity in the twenties when the Hallé Orchestra, conducted by Hamilton Harty, visited Dublin three times.[39] In 1927 an attempt was made to revive the Dublin Orchestral Society with conductors Michele Esposito and John Larchet. In the same year, the Dublin Philharmonic Society was established, coinciding with the foundation of the radio station 2RN, which led to the eventual formation of a studio orchestra by Vincent O'Brien.[40] These initiatives were beneficial for Irish composers, whose works were broadcast and given public performances.

In 1926 Boyle sent the scores of *The Magic Harp* and *Colin Clout* to Colonel Fritz Brase, conductor of the Dublin Philharmonic Society. At last, on 16 March 1929, *The Magic Harp* was given its first Dublin performance at an afternoon concert of the Society in the Theatre Royal, which combined the forces of the Dublin Symphony Orchestra and the Dublin Philharmonic Choral Society. Of the sixty-nine members of the orchestra, twenty-six came from the Army Band. Brase autographed the copy of the score of *The Magic Harp* with a complimentary inscription: 'Mit grossem Vernügen habe ich dieses schöne und interessante Werk dirigiert' [I have conducted this beautiful and interesting work with great pleasure]. The souvenir programme for the concert lists no fewer than thirty-seven Vice-Presidents of the Dublin Philharmonic Society, including Boyle's old teacher, Samuel S. Myerscough, and Dr George Hewson. The concert lasted two and a half hours, and included two works by Brahms – the 'Tragic' overture and the *German Requiem* – and the Good Friday music from *Parsifal*. The choral conductor was Turner Huggard, who had played the organ at Woodbrook in 1920 at another significant event in Boyle's life, the premiere of *Soldiers at Peace* by Bray Choral Society. In his analytical notes on the programme Harold R. White[41] stated:

> This remarkable rhapsody for orchestra was chosen for publication in the Carnegie Collection of British music. Its composer is an Irish lady – a pupil of Dr Kitson to whom the work is dedicated. It is scored for a large orchestra including corno Inglese, bass clarinet, tuba and harp … The themes are treated with skill and power. Miss Boyle shows not only great facility in counterpoint, but a fine sense of colour in orchestration, which combined with her command of rhythm and knowledge of instrumental technique, renders her work worthy of respect, and places the composer high in the ranks of Irish musicians.

The review in *The Irish Times* was equally favourable:

> Miss Boyle's work, dedicated to Dr Kitson, with whom she has studied, is highly effective music for full orchestra, exhibiting abundant beauty of theme and of instrumental treatment. The composer was called to the platform at its conclusion and applauded with deserved heartiness. Devoid of extravagances, her music shows due appreciation of modern orchestral resources. Its poetical theme is drawn from Irish folk-lore.[42]

The headline on the *Irish Independent* proclaimed:

'THE MAGIC HARP'
LADY COMPOSER'S WORK

The programme included 'The Magic Harp', a rhapsody which is the work of Miss Ina Boyle, an Irish composer. It is a well-conceived work, inspired by an old Irish legend, and is remarkable for the pithiness of its main themes, which are skilfully worked out and harmonised with much originality. Miss Boyle has used almost all the resources of the modern orchestra in scoring the work, and such is her fine sense of orchestral colour that it is nowhere overburdened with tone.[43]

The *Daily Mail* report outdid the local accounts:

RHAPSODY OF COLOUR
FEATURES OF FINE DUBLIN CONCERT
From our special correspondent
Dublin, Saturday
Pandora must have contemplated opening her magic box in much the same state of mind as that in which one approached the performance this afternoon of Miss Ina Boyle's Magic Harp rhapsody by Dublin Philharmonic Society Orchestra. The rhapsody, itself an admirable box of tricks, is the work of an Irishwoman and was chosen for publication in the Carnegie collection of British music. Colonel Fritz Brase's young orchestra is little used to such remarkable works. Miss Boyle has drenched her rhapsody in highly coloured dyes and has harnessed beams of artificial sunlight to the task of irradiating themes which might have relied more on their own poetic beauty. The glowing colours of the piece – for what they are intrinsically worth – were perfectly painted by Colonel Brase and his orchestra.[44]

The adulation continued in H. F. Norman's review in *The Irish Statesman*:

A German Requiem and an Irish Rhapsody
I must give my remaining space to a remarkable – and this is scarcely to our credit – first-time performance in Dublin (in Ireland, indeed save for a Belfast broadcast of a Dublin lady's 'Rhapsody'), 'The Magic Harp' has been performed with success under both Adrian Boult and Sir Henry Wood in London; it is time her own country honoured Miss Boyle. The fabled harp played by the wind among the apple-trees, with its iron string for sleep, bronze for laughter, silver for weeping, works out 'according to programme' in three movements. I liked best to receive it, however, as abstract music. Simple without obviousness, or distinctive without studied complexity, it gives each branch of the orchestra scope. It is not 'folky', and yet I think one would trace its geographical origins to Ireland. And – yet again – however accordant with the spirit of our island, primeval, natural, made of Irish air and wind, it is cosmopolitan in its cultural catholicity. May I suggest that it be played again soon? Irish

people should learn to know more of their own composers, not least of those women of talent of whom Miss Boyle is the latest.[45]

A month after the concert Boyle sent Brase the score of the '*Glencree*' symphony at his request. The complete work had never been performed and there was a prospect of including it in the Dublin Philharmonic Society autumn season. Brase said it 'seemed very interesting, especially the scherzo, but he had not definitely decided his programme'. In the event it was not chosen, but *The Magic Harp* was given another performance in November at an afternoon concert in the RDS. On this occasion, Harold R. White was less enthusiastic: 'Miss Ina Boyle's rhapsody, "The Magic Harp", shows an original vein of melody, some daring splashes of orchestral colour, and is interesting for its detail rather than from its general structure. The performance was marred by the harp being out of tune.'[46]

The Dublin Philharmonic Orchestra lapsed after 1936 and as the Radio Station orchestra had only twenty-four members in 1935 there was little scope for orchestral performances in Dublin. In 1934, Aloys Fleischmann, newly appointed professor of music at University College Cork, had established a University Orchestra (later the Cork Symphony Orchestra). The orchestra gave regular public concerts in Cork, which were broadcast by Radio Éireann. A significant feature of the concerts was the inclusion on the programme of at least one work by an Irish composer.[47] On 1 April 1936 there was an overflow audience in the university's Aula Maxima for a concert by the sixty-strong orchestra, at which Boyle's revised version of *Colin Clout* was performed. After the concert a full account of the composer's career, headed by a studio photograph, appeared in a feature article, 'Rambling Reflections' by 'Omnibus' in *The Cork Examiner*:

> I like the ambition of the Cork University Orchestra to bring the works of rising Irish composers before the music-loving public ... At the most recent of the concerts of this local ensemble another orchestral composition by an Irish composer was forthcoming – this time a pastoral from a young lady who appears to have a great future before her in the musical world. She is Miss Ina Boyle of Enniskerry, Co. Wicklow and the composition was 'Colin Clout', a fragrant and very competent affair for large orchestra. This was really a most outstanding memory for those who heard the orchestra last week – a beautiful work beautifully given. Miss Boyle has studied composition under Vaughan Williams and her works which include a violin concerto, two symphonies and several suites, have

been frequently performed by the BBC. I expect to hear more of Miss Boyle both on the wireless and on the platform – and perhaps in the annals of music.[48]

The review in the *Evening Echo* (sister paper of *The Cork Examiner*) reported with some local pride:

> This latest effort of the orchestra, however, impressed as an improvement on anything previously attempted – a fact which seemed to strike the audience right at the start when the ensemble was at the first movement of Pastoral 'Colin Clout', the work of Miss Ina Boyle of Enniskerry. 'Colin Clout' is a charming work of its kind – a work of changing moods which the orchestra caught from the first complaining wail of the flute to the tranquillity and quiet of the concluding passages. Betwixt beginning and end Miss Boyle contrived to tell the story of a love-lorn shepherd in its varying moods, and excellently her story was recounted last night. This was the first time one of her works was produced in Cork and indeed she is a fortunate young lady to have her pastoral – an exquisite piece – placed in the hands of a combination capable of transmitting the mood of her poem to the listeners.[49]

Two years later Fleischmann came to Dublin to conduct the Radio Éireann Orchestra in the final concert of a series of four celebrity concerts in the Gaiety Theatre. The concert on 24 April was a ground-breaking event, consisting entirely of music by Irish composers. *Colin Clout* shared the programme with the first performance in Ireland of Elizabeth Maconchy's pianoforte concertino (1930), with Charles Lynch as soloist, and works by Frederick May, E. J. Moeran, Hamilton Harty and Muiris Ó Rónáin (Fleischmann's pseudonym). A preview of the concert with photographs of the composers was headed 'Ireland has her composers'.[50] Philip Dore summed up the occasion in *The Irish Times*:

> I have no recollection in recent years of such interest being taken in a musical function in any way comparable with that of the Orchestral Concert in the Gaiety Theatre on Sunday afternoon. And justifiably so for the project was a courageous one and of a nature certain to stimulate the interest of most, and to ensure the attendance of a large and representative audience. From the beginning of Ina Boyle's Pastorale 'Colin Clout' it was apparent that the promoters of the concert had made no promises that they did not intend to fulfil, for here was sane well-poised music

given a performance that had every evidence of careful and meticulous preparation.[51]

A feature article by Kitty Clive focused on the two women composers:

> I am particularly interested that two brilliant Irishwomen will be represented on the programme. It seems, indeed, strange that while they are both from the suburbs of Dublin few know anything about them and their work. But Miss Elizabeth Maconchy and Miss Ina Boyle have already had their compositions given in the music centres of the Continent, and now for the first time in Ireland we shall hear the work of six Irish composers, and all will be present on the platform except Sir Hamilton Harty, who is unable to attend through illness but gives his blessing to the concert.

At a time when women composers were seen and not heard the writer continued: 'And who are the two women whose works we will hear? They are both very modest about their achievements and diffident to speak for themselves relying on the response they make through their music.'[52]

The end of a chapter

The outbreak of the Second World War had put an end to Boyle's travels to London. It was also the end of a chapter in her life that had given her encouragement as a composer and had reinforced her determination to have her music performed. Over a period of sixteen years she had gained the friendship of Vaughan Williams and through him had made contact with other prominent musicians. He had welcomed her into his home, had given her introductions to influential figures and had taken her seriously as a composer. In addition, he had acted as her mentor in dealing with publishers and had suggested performers for her works.

During that time she had enjoyed concerts at the Royal College of Music, the Queen's Hall and the Aeolian Hall and had attended opera and ballet performances. She had visited the British Museum and had become familiar with the London, literary and musical scene. After the war she continued to visit London where several of her works were performed at concerts held by the Macnaghten New Music Group, of which Vaughan Williams was President, but there is no record of any further lessons with him. His first wife, Adeline, was virtually an invalid until her death in 1951, and after his re-marriage to Ursula Woods in 1953 he moved from Dorking to a house at 10 Hanover Terrace, NW1. In 1958 Boyle received a typed postcard from this address:

> Miss Boyle
> Sir Malcolm Sargent is running through my new symphony at St. Pancras Town Hall on 21 March.[53] The session will last from 2.30 p.m. till 5.30 p.m. He will rehearse from 2.30 p.m. to 4 p.m. & run right through at about 4.15 p.m.
> I should be very glad if you would come. Please bring this card with you.
> [handwritten] Yrs RWV
> R.S.V.P.

Three months after the premiere of his last symphony Ralph Vaughan Williams died on 26 August 1958. In December, Ina Boyle wrote a Christmas letter to her neighbour Sheila Wingfield,[54] which ended: 'I have no musical news. I was in London for a few days to hear the rehearsal of Vaughan Williams' 9th symphony and I saw him there, but knew I never should do so again, though he was quite unchanged to talk to.'[55]

3

A Changing World

New friendships

During her visits to London, Boyle was fortunate to meet a remarkable group of women who, although they belonged to a younger generation, became her friends and gave her valuable support for the rest of her life. These included composers Elizabeth Maconchy and Grace Williams, both pupils of Vaughan Williams, and Anne Macnaghten and Iris Lemare, who, together with Elizabeth Lutyens, founded the Macnaghten/Lemare Concerts in 1931, which provided a platform for music by contemporary composers. Boyle and Maconchy already knew one another; their families were friends. Elizabeth lived in Dublin until she was sixteen, when she left to study at the RCM; her first teacher there was Charles Wood, who was married to Boyle's cousin, Charlotte. Although there was an age difference of eighteen years between the two women, their literary and intellectual tastes were similar and both were deeply committed to composition.

At that time women composers faced many challenges from concert promoters and publishers. Boosey & Hawkes told Maconchy that they would not consider publishing orchestral music by 'a young lady, perhaps a few songs'. She was realistic about the problems that confronted women composers: 'It was difficult for a woman to make a career as a composer in the 30s – there was still plenty of anti-feminine prejudice, especially among concert promoters and publishers.'[1] In her 'Memoranda', Boyle provides numerous examples of assistance that she received from Maconchy. In 1931 she went through the *Virgilian Suite* carefully and gave her many useful hints about the scoring. Other works that she looked at while Boyle was still taking lessons from Vaughan Williams included her overture for orchestra, *Seven Psalms*, *The Vision of Er* and the string quartet. Sometimes the situation was reversed, as in June 1934, when Maconchy wrote: 'I shall of course be most delighted to go and see you all at Bushey and I will bring my musical efforts with me to show you what I have done in the way of polishing – and I hope improvements.'[2]

Boyle left instructions in her will for her trustee to consult Elizabeth LeFanu (née Maconchy) 'as to all matters relating to her music as she is the only person who is intimately acquainted with it and my wishes about it'. In August 1967, Maconchy listed Boyle's manuscript scores in a small green notebook under four categories: orchestral, choral, chamber music and opera. This was the genesis of her personal tribute – *Ina Boyle*: *An Appreciation with a Select List of her Music* – which was published by the Dolmen Press for Trinity College Dublin in 1974. The chosen works were categorised as 'most suited for performance and suitable for capable amateurs as well as professionals'.

The Welsh composer Grace Williams (1906–1977) was another friend, who helped Boyle both musically and professionally. In November 1933 when Boyle sent her extracts from her cantata *Christ is a path* (1925), which had been rejected by the Carnegie Fund, Grace recommended it to the Director of the BBC at Cardiff. To Boyle's delight three numbers from the work were broadcast on 27 June 1935 with Beatrice Pugh, soprano, as soloist in 'a most charming first performance'. Grace later looked at the overture for orchestra and during the war Maconchy lent her the score of *The Vision of Er*. When she sent a long criticism of the latter, Boyle placed the notes in the original score, adding rather cryptically: 'I may adopt some of her suggestions when I can get both scores together.'

Anne Macnaghten (1908–2000) also had Irish roots. She came from a privileged background; her father was Sir Malcolm Macnaghten KBE, MP for Londonderry 1922–28, and Judge of the High Court, King's Bench Division from 1928 to 1947. She was a violinist and had studied in Leipzig and in London, where she was advised to concentrate on chamber music. In 1931 she founded the Macnaghten String Quartet and together with Elizabeth Lutyens and Iris Lemare organised a series of chamber music concerts of mostly contemporary music in the Ballet Club Theatre, Notting Hill Gate. The concerts were an instant success, supported by composers and their friends, in particular with help and encouragement from Vaughan Williams. In a letter to Macnaghten in 1932 he wrote: 'You are doing great work and putting the B.B.C. and T. Beecham to shame.'[3] The concerts were discontinued in 1937 but were resumed in 1950 and lasted until 1978.

In 1931 Boyle asked Anne to include her *Five Sacred Sicilian Folksongs* in the Macnaghten–Lemare concerts but they were not considered suitable. She made numerous attempts to have her string quartet performed by the Macnaghten Quartet and they rehearsed it in March 1935. A year later Iris Lemare showed it to the Stratton Quartet but they did not play it, so it was returned to Anne. At last, on 15 July 1937, it was broadcast by the Macnaghten Quartet, who also recorded it at Memphis Recording Studios Ltd, 131 Wigmore Street, on 10 November 1937. The members of the quartet were Anne Macnaghten (1st violin), Elise Desprez (2nd violin), Phyllis Chapman (viola) and Olive Richards (cello).[4]

Boyle's setting for tenor and string quartet of John Donne's *Thinke then, my soule* was another work that she showed to Anne Macnaghten. Anne rehearsed it with the quartet in June 1938 and suggested Jan van der Gucht as soloist. She gave the singer a copy of the score, but he was not available when Boyle was in London in November. Unfortunately, the proposed performance was affected by the threat of war and uncertainty in the wake of the Munich Agreement. In a postscript to a letter to Sheila Wingfield, Boyle reported that she had a letter from Anne Macnaghten 'saying that she had to put off the concert at which she meant to have played my "Donne" on account of the crisis, but she still means to do it later'.[5] After the rehearsal Boyle had revised the work and she submitted it to the ISCM on two successive years, but it was not accepted. She later showed it to Vaughan Williams when he visited Bushey Park.

Her sister Phyllis, who was bedridden for several years due to a heart ailment, died after a short illness on 21 July 1938.[6] Boyle paid the cost of publication of the work by OUP from Phyllis's 'fowl money, as her present to me'. She then sent copies to Jan van der Gucht, Steuart Wilson, André Mangeot and Vaughan Williams, and eventually it was broadcast by the BBC on 16 December 1942 by Harold Bradbury and the Zorian Quartet. It was also performed on 3 May 1945 by René Soames and the Hirsch Quartet from Beverley Minster, in the fifth of a series of concerts from historic buildings, organised by the BBC and CEMA,[7] and in 1952 at the Ladies' Musical Society in Oxford with David Galliver as soloist.

Extended family

Boyle had several cousins from both sides of her family living in England. These included her mother's nieces, Ina (Selina) Jephson[8] and her sister Adelaide,[9] daughters of Henry Lorenzo Jephson JP (1845–1914), who had been a member of London County Council, and Adelaide's children, Brigadier Arthur Fortescue MBE MC, and his sister Diana. Another cousin, Charles Wood's widow Charlotte, who was living in Cambridge, helped to promote her music.

In 1936 she showed two of Boyle's choral works, 'Holy art Thou' and 'Jesu that dear boughtest thee', to Heathcoat Statham, an ex-pupil of Wood, reader at publishers Deane & Co., who suggested their suitability for the Three Choirs Festival.

Her Boyle cousins, whose father had died in 1919, had moved with their mother from Belmont House, Rathdowney, County Laois, in 1922 to Ross-on-Wye, Herefordshire, when Doreen, the youngest of the family, was only eleven years old. She went to school in Malvern, where she studied the violin, and later played with the City of Birmingham Symphony Orchestra from July 1944 to May 1946. Doreen's eldest sister, Sylvia Duckworth, had married in 1920 and was living in Ross-on-Wye, where her husband was a doctor. Their eldest brother, Dermot,[10] who was educated in St Columba's College, Rathfarnham, entered the newly established RAF College at Cranwell at the age of eighteen, in 1922, the same year that his cousin's orchestral work *Colin Clout* was given its first performance in London.

The vibrant London musical scene at that time offered Boyle opportunities to hear music far beyond her Dublin horizons. In the cover of one of her notebooks she preserved newspaper cuttings of advertisements for concerts held in London during the 1922–23 season. They included subscription concerts by the New Queen's Hall Orchestra, conducted by Henry Wood, the seventeenth series of LSO concerts, conducted by Albert Coates and Koussevitzky, and Eugene Goosens' Chamber Music Concerts in the Aeolian Hall, where popular repertoire was combined with premieres of exciting new works by living composers. During her subsequent visits to London she continued to avail of every opportunity to attend concerts.

War years

During the war, Elizabeth Maconchy provided safekeeping at Downton Castle, Ludlow, for some of Boyle's scores which could not be posted to Ireland, and also acted as intermediary between her and publishers and other agencies. In 1941 Boyle sent her a copy of the full score and the piano arrangement of a new work, *Hellas*, for soprano solo, chorus and orchestra, a sequence of epitaphs 'in memory of those who died for Greece'. She asked her to send it to Hubert Foss at OUP when she had looked at it. Unfortunately, although they sent a 'nice letter' back, the publishers could not take new works owing to the paper shortage. She then asked them to send it to the BBC, who rejected it, but asked to see other compositions and returned the score to Maconchy for the duration of the war.[11]

In 1997, Nicola LeFanu, daughter of Elizabeth Maconchy, presented a miscellaneous collection of Boyle's sketches, manuscripts and printed music dating from 1922 to 1966 to the Library of Trinity College Dublin. It included a copy of the four-part motet, *O Thou! Whose Spirit*, inscribed 'Betty from Ina 19 December 1940', and the settings of three songs by Walter de la Mare, dated 1 July 1956, with the caption 'Betty with love from Ina'. Boyle had also become close to her cousin Doreen Boyle, as the only other member of the family who was a professional musician. In 1939 she gave her the scores of the string quartet[12] and the violin concerto, both of which were returned after the war.

At this time there was a reduction in Boyle's creativity and her rate of composition was waning. She missed the stimulation of the London musical scene and her friends in England. For the second time in her life she was deeply affected by war. In 1940 she returned to one of her favourite poets, Winifred M. Letts, for a setting of her poem 'Easter snow', in memory of a friend who had died. The text for 'Faith', an elegiac song for tenor, string quartet, flute and harp (1941), was taken from words published in *The Daily Telegraph* by an anonymous flight lieutenant whose elder brother had been killed on active service on Christmas Eve. Back in Dublin she approached Cepta Cullen of the Irish Ballet Company to discuss a production of *The Dance of Death* at the Peacock Theatre, but nothing came of it.

Rev. Canon Kingsmill Moore, who had selected the text for *The Transfiguration*, the work that had brought her local recognition twenty years earlier, celebrated his ninetieth birthday on 11 December 1942. She had not written any orchestral music since 1936, but her sketch for small orchestra, *Wildgeese*, inspired by the flight of geese over Lough Bray, was dedicated to him in honour of the occasion. A quotation from Alcaeus is given on the title page: 'What birds are these which have come from the ends of the earth and the ocean / Wildgeese of motley neck and widespread wing?' She sent a copy of the score to the BBC, but it was rejected. She also sent it to Henry Wood, who returned it to Maconchy until the war was over.

Music in Dublin

During the war, there was a resurgence of interest in classical music in Dublin. When Lieutenant (later Captain) Michael Bowles,[13] on secondment from the Irish Army, was appointed conductor of the Radio Éireann Orchestra on 1 January 1941, there were only twenty-six regular members so brass and wind players from the Army bands were brought in to swell the ranks.[14] With the support of Séamus Ó Braonáin, Director of Broadcasting, and R. J. Cremins, assistant secretary of the Department of Posts and Telegraphs, Bowles initiated a highly successful series of fortnightly public concerts in the Mansion House.[15]

In 1942 the orchestra was expanded to forty professional players. Studio concerts in the Scots Church Hall, Abbey Street, were open to the public, and from 1943 concerts were held on Sunday afternoons in the Capitol Theatre, O'Connell Street, which had a seating capacity of 2,300. The Minister for Posts and Telegraphs, P. J. Little TD, and the secretary of the Department, Léon Ó Broin, actively encouraged the development of music in the national broadcasting service. Music by Irish composers was regularly performed, and Boyle sent copies of her scores to the Radio Éireann music librarian at the GPO Studios in Henry Street, for the attention of conductors.

Dr Arthur Duff,[16] who had been conductor of the No. 2 Army Band in Cork before he joined Radio Éireann, is frequently mentioned in her 'Memoranda'. On 22 January 1944, he conducted a concert of Boyle's compositions that was broadcast in the 'Irish Composers' series.[17] The programme included both *The Magic Harp* and *Colin Clout*. The Prelude and Finale from her masque *The Dance of Death* were also scheduled, but the orchestral parts were not ready in time, so the first movement of the '*Glencree*' symphony was played instead. The concert was also notable for the first performance of her more recent work, *Wildgeese*, with soloist Clyde Twelvetrees, formerly principal cellist of the Hallé Orchestra, who had settled in Dublin and had joined the expanded RÉ orchestra. A year later the '*Glencree*' symphony was given its first complete performance at a studio concert conducted by Arthur Duff.[18]

In 1944, Arthur Hutchings, professor of music at the University of Durham, welcomed Boyle's edition of a song by Purcell in a review in *The Musical Times* of new music published by OUP:

> It is good to see no impoverishment of paper for the issue of Purcell's 'With sick and famished eyes' though the price asked is less than that of many an ephemeral ballad. Purcell's setting of Herbert's 'Longing' was included in Playford's 'Harmonia Sacra', 1688, and scored for voice with theorbo-lute, bass viol, and harpsichord or organ. This is good sincere Purcell in the recitative style which without ever becoming arioso achieves its own formal unity. Ina Boyle edits the song for keyboard, voice and 'cello. It is hoped that her taste and skill will be employed on further undertakings of this nature. Small type notes are supplied in the piano part for use when no 'cello is present.[19]

Meanwhile another work with a Greek theme brought unexpected rewards. When Harold Bradbury asked her to write something for him, Boyle chose a translation from the Greek of a third-century poem for a chamber work, *Lament for Bion* (1944–45). She wrote the first version for tenor and string orchestra and sent it to Radio Éireann for a proposed programme of her works, which was postponed because the soloist, Robert McCullagh, was not available. Then she gave a string quartet version to Harold Bradbury and lent another copy to Elizabeth Maconchy. Next she sent the score to the ISCM for inspection, but it was returned in 1946. However, when she entered it for the Olympic Art Competition, held in conjunction with the Olympic Games in London in 1948, she received a commemoration medal and a *Diplôme d'Honneur* in the music category.[20] From 1932 a new classification of 'Honourable Mention' had been added for works that in the opinion of the jury deserved a commendation. The Chairman of the Music Committee was Arnold Bax.

4

Post War

Compositions and performances

As life returned to normal after the war, Boyle resumed composition with a setting for bass solo and orchestra of *The Prophet* (1946), with text from Pushkin, translated by Maurice Baring. It was a substantial work, but her efforts to have it performed or published were unsuccessful. In 1947 a new series of programmes, 'Music by Contemporary Irish Composers', was announced, to be broadcast on Radio Éireann on seven consecutive Monday nights. The first programme was devoted to music by Boyle. She was the only female composer represented, the other composers featured in the series being Brian Boydell, John Beckett, Daniel McNulty, Havelock Nelson, Michael Bowles and Charles O'Donnell Sweeney.[1] The programme included *Hymne To God my God, in my sicknesse* (1946), which she had written for her father's eighty-sixth birthday, performed by tenor Robert McCullagh and the Cuala Quartet; and four songs – 'Eternity', 'A song of enchantment', 'A song of shadows' and 'Sleep Song' – sung by soprano Jean Nolan, accompanied by Rhoda Coghill, station accompanist.[2]

The end of the war had brought an influx of European musicians to Dublin, both as members of the RÉSO and as soloists. By 1948 the orchestra had been enlarged to sixty-two members (including a pianist), and there was also a Light Orchestra with twenty-two players. The Phoenix Hall in Dublin city centre was renovated for studio concerts, with seats for an audience of 300–400. The young French conductor Jean Martinon conducted symphony concerts in Dublin from 1946, and tutored in orchestral conducting at the Department of Education Summer School, which was held in conjunction with Radio Éireann. In 1947 and 1948 he also taught composition at the course, which Boyle attended.[3]

According to her 'Memoranda' she gave Martinon several scores – including *The Vision of Er* and *The Dance of Death* – to choose from for a broadcast. In the end he selected Overture for orchestra (1933–34) and it was performed at a studio concert in the Phoenix Hall on 27 February 1948. Among the other works on the programme was Stravinsky's *Pulcinella*. There was also a reminder of the past when the choral lecturer at the Summer School, her old friend Charles Kennedy Scott – who had first performed four of the *Gaelic Hymns* in London in 1931 with the Oriana Madrigal Society – conducted the Summer School choir in 'The soul leading', with Jean Nolan as soloist.[4]

There were other signs that her music was gaining wider recognition. Edmond Appia, of the Orchestre de la Suisse Romande, who was guest conductor of the RÉSO from October 1947 until January 1948, conducted *Wildgeese* at a studio concert in the Phoenix Hall on 18 November 1947. It was repeated at Appia's final symphony concert in the Capitol Theatre on 25 January 1948, in a programme of works by Pergolesi, Beethoven, Lalo and Chabrier. Both concerts were broadcast.[5] She also showed the scores of several of her works to another visiting conductor, Mosco Carner, while he was in Dublin, and posted the score of *Hellas* to his London address, but no performance ensued. However, two of the *Gaelic Hymns* were heard at concerts during the year. On 28 January 1948 'The soul leading' was relayed by Radio Éireann from a concert by the Tramore Singers at Waterford Music Club,[6] while on 29 June 'The light'ner of the stars' was performed by the Oriana Madrigal Society in the Wigmore Hall.

When the Korean conductor Ahn Eak Tai (1906–65) conducted a concert in Dublin on 20 February 1938, Boyle sent him a copy of the score and a set of orchestral parts of Overture for orchestra. In 1949 he conducted two of her earlier works, *The Magic Harp* and *Colin Clout*, at concerts in Teatro Principal, *Palma de Mallorca*, by the Orquesta Sinfonica de Mallorca. There is no evidence that the composer attended but she kept seven copies of one of the programmes and two Spanish newspaper reviews with her papers.[7] Earlier in that year, Arthur Duff conducted *Wildgeese* for the third time at a studio concert by the RÉSO in the Phoenix Hall.[8] There were two other first performances ahead in Dublin, both conducted by her fellow composer Brian Boydell. On 4 October 1949, a movement from *The Vision of Er* was performed by the Radio Éireann Symphony Orchestra,[9] while on 30 November 1950, *Elegy* from the *Virgilian Suite* was played at a concert by the Dublin Orchestral Players in the Metropolitan Hall, Abbey Street.[10]

Joseph O'Neill, music critic of the *Irish Independent*, was particularly impressed by the performance of the former work:

In spite of the absence of the stage setting the music was able to stand as a concert item of programme style. The picture of the arid plain of Lethe is faithfully drawn and there is dramatic force in the change of mood which indicates the drinking of the waters of oblivion. There is a fine clarity in Ina Boyle's orchestral writing and her musical ideas are logically expressed. Brian Boydell secured a colourful performance of the work. The flute solo playing was expressive of the scene in the opening section.[11]

From the Darkness

It was at this time that Boyle launched into an undertaking that was to prove one of the most painful episodes of her professional life, the composition of her third symphony, for contralto and orchestra, *From the Darkness* (1946–51). There were three movements, with text selected from the poetry of Edith Sitwell: I 'Invocation', II 'An Old Woman' and III 'Harvest'. Possessing a strong affinity with Sitwell's poetry she was also working on a setting of her poem depicting the bombing of London, 'Still falls the rain'. Unfortunately, she had not contacted the poet in advance to ask permission to use the texts. In February 1952, she sent a two-page letter requesting Sitwell's permission to set the texts, together with the scores.

> I fully understand that it would be a great favour if you allowed me to use extracts from three most beautiful poems, yet the three together seem to me so symphonic in effect that I hope you may consider it.[12]

A few days later Boyle received a postcard from J. F. Robins, Edith Sitwell's butler, asking whether he should return the manuscripts to her, as Dr Sitwell was in Italy for at least two months. Later he sent a telegram with the name of the hotel where she was staying in Amalfi, but, when Boyle wrote to her, permission was graciously but firmly refused:

> I am deeply sorry to be obliged to say to anyone as charming as you obviously are, that I cannot give permission for these settings. But with regard to 'Still falls the rain' I am under a contract that makes it impossible, and I cannot, I am afraid, see my way to giving you permission for the other poems either. It is only under the very rarest circumstances that I like my poems to be set, and I can never allow them to be cut, even under those circumstances. I am so sorry. It is sad and disappointing to work in vain. It is always best really to write to me first, before setting the poems.[13]

The refusal was disappointing for Boyle, especially as Edith Sitwell had returned the music unopened. Boyle wrote an alternative text herself and copied it into the vocal score, but in the end she did not use it because she felt the loss of the original poems was too great. Having wasted six years on the project she decided that the work would never be performed. Soon after Edith Sitwell attended the first performance of Benjamin Britten's setting of 'Still falls the rain', Sheila Wingfield wrote:

> It is infuriating and tragic that Edith Sitwell should have allowed him and not you to set her words – If only you had been less modest and approached her with a proper fanfare and let her know your worth, but what's the use now.[14]

The ban imposed by Edith Sitwell in 1952 was confirmed by Sitwell's literary executors. However, in 1975 Elizabeth Maconchy was successful in having the prohibition lifted and permission granted for both works to be published or performed.

The Music Association of Ireland

In 1948 Boyle joined the newly formed Music Association of Ireland (MAI), whose council included composers Brian Boydell, Aloys Fleischmann, Frederick May and Edgar Deale. In response to a circular sent in advance of the first meeting she wrote: 'I regret that I cannot attend the proposed meeting as I live so far from Dublin that I find it impossible to get to the evening meetings.'[15] She also queried one of the aims of the Association, listed on the circular, which proposed detaching musical policy from Civil Service control.

> The Civil Service have the most money and power to help music, and there has been a good deal done in the last year or two, as in establishing the Summer School of Music, the enlarging and improving of the Radio Orchestra, and the provision of the Phoenix Hall that could hardly have been done privately.[16]

As a result of her intervention the wording was changed to 'the advising of the Ministers concerned on musical policy generally'.[17] When an inaugural meeting was held on 30 October 1949 only a few composers attended, but letters and telephone calls were received afterwards from about twenty others who welcomed the idea of forming a body to look after their specific interests.

In 1953 a Composers' Group was set up within the MAI which, it was hoped, would develop into a national representative body – an Irish branch of the ISCM.[18] Boyle suggested that a catalogue of music by Irish composers should be published giving short particulars of works for international information.[19] Twenty years later, a year after her death, a catalogue of works by twenty-three contemporary Irish composers was published by the MAI.[20] It included only five of her compositions: *The Magic Harp*, *Hellas*, *Thinke then, my soule*, *No coward soul is mine* and five *Gaelic Hymns*. The second edition of the catalogue, published in 1973, devoted seven pages to a comprehensive list of her works under eleven categories.[21]

After her father's death at the age of ninety-one, in November 1951, Boyle had more freedom to travel and more time for composition. As she entered her sixties she concentrated on vocal music, creating a cantata for soprano, chorus and organ: 'Blessed be the Lord for He hath showed me His marvellous kindness' (1952–54). In 1953 she set *Three Mediaeval Latin Lyrics* (tr. Helen Waddell) – 'Sleep', 'Storm' and 'Evening on the Moselle' – for Sophie Wyss, soprano, but the music did not arrive in time for the concert for which they were intended. She sent her six-part motet *The spacious firmament on high* (1954) to Charles Kennedy Scott, who accepted it for the Oriana Madrigal Society. Sixty photo-facsimile copies were made but to her disappointment he did not like it at rehearsal and it was dropped from the programme.[22] On 29 April 1954, Patricia Thomas, contralto, accompanied by Rhoda Coghill, included 'A song of enchantment' in the second of three programmes of 'Songs by Contemporary Irish Composers' broadcast by Radio Éireann.

Macnaghten concerts

Some of Boyle's works were given their first performances at the Macnaghten New Music Group concerts, which were revived in London in 1950. On 4 April 1955, *Three Mediaeval Latin Lyrics* (1953) and *Two Songs of the Woods* (1954) were performed by Joan Gray, mezzo-soprano, at a concert in the Drawing Room of the Arts Council of Great Britain. They were perceptively reviewed by Donald Mitchell:

> Miss Boyle is an Irish composer who has studied with Vaughan Williams. Her songs, to words by Meredith and Latin lyrics translated by Helen Waddell, were very conservative in style and strongly influenced by her teacher. They were the kind of 'English' song Vaughan Williams himself was writing as a young man. Nevertheless, Miss Boyle's songs, but for

the embarrassingly whimsical ones, gave me some enjoyment. They were competently done and not without real feeling, for example the touching 'Dirge in the Woods'. The accompaniments played by Eric Stevens were well laid out, especially in 'Storm', an effective song which should find favour with recitalists who seek something unadventurous but not dull. A tiny breath of feeling will go a long way to postpone the date when a regressively orthodox idiom becomes finally outdated.[23]

In 1956, when two *Gaelic Hymns* were scheduled to be performed by the Purcell Singers at a Macnaghten concert,[24] Sheila Wingfield encouraged her friend to attend in spite of her farming commitments: 'do go and hear your music and let the thresher thresh in your absence'.[25]

In Dublin, Boyle's orchestral works were occasionally included in RÉSO programmes. Milan Horvat conducted *Wildgeese* at a winter 'Prom' concert in the Gaiety Theatre on 9 January 1955, which was broadcast the following week.[26] In her 'Memoranda' she reports that she sent the inscribed full score of *The Magic Harp* to the RÉSO Librarian for inspection by Horvat. He did not conduct it himself, but later in the year Éimear Ó Broin included the work in a concert in the Abbey Lecture Hall, which was subsequently broadcast.[27] The review of the concert stated succinctly: 'The Magic Harp is as aptly scored as it is titled.'[28] She also continued her efforts to promote her music in England. In 1957 she sent the score of *Wildgeese* to Maconchy to play it for Vaughan Williams. He spoke of sending it to John Barbirolli but, when after a year she inquired from the Hallé secretary, she found that it had never been sent, and in March 1958 it was returned to her by Ursula Vaughan Williams.

Boyle had circulated the score of another work, a setting of Emily Bronte's poem 'No coward soul is mine' (1953), for contralto and string orchestra, to several English musicians. She sent it to Meredith Davies, organist, for consideration for the Three Choirs Festival, and to Dr Paul Steinitz, founder of the London Bach Society, but without success. The work was finally performed at a concert of Contemporary Women Composers (Antoinette Kirkwood, Elizabeth Maconchy, Grace Williams, Ruth Gipps, Dorothy Howell and Ina Boyle) at the Wigmore Hall on 28 April 1960. The Kathleen Merrett Orchestra, 'mainly masculine', was conducted by Kathleen Merrett and the soloist was Janet Baker. According to the review in *The Musical Times* by Stanley Bayliss:

'Contemporary' is a much abused word nowadays, but all six ladies, I am glad to say, are living and five of them took 'calls'. Not one of their works, however, could be regarded as stylistically contemporary …

The most notable works were Elizabeth Maconchy's *Concertino* and Grace Williams's *Sea Sketches*, but neither attained real individuality or memorability, both being reflective of Vaughan Williams ... Ina Boyle's setting of Emily Bronte's 'No coward soul is mine' made the mistake of converting a poem that is essentially a personal avowal into a platform harangue. Surely this particular poem does not call at all for music? ... Nothing in this programme lodged in the memory as do fragments from Ethel Smyth's *The Wreckers*, *The Boatswain's Mate*, and *Fête Galante*. Incidentally Dame Ethel would not have approved of this segregation of women composers![29]

In 1953, Anne Macnaghten moved house from London to Saffron Walden in Essex. It was there that Boyle's setting of *Still falls the rain* was recorded in 1964 by Margaret Cable, mezzo-soprano, and the Macnaghten Quartet (Anne Macnaghten, Bernard Blay, Pauline Jackson and Arnold Ashby). Another chamber work, *Three Songs by Ben Jonson* (1955), for mezzo-soprano, violin and cello, composed for Anne Macnaghten and her second husband Arnold Ashby, was recorded at the same time. The tape recordings were subsequently processed as 33⅓ records by HMV at Eamonn Andrews Studios, Dublin.[30]

In 1956 Boyle returned to one of her favourite poets, Walter de la Mare, for three songs which she dedicated to her cousin Ina Jephson. She also revised a setting of *Three Ancient Irish Poems*, translated by Kuno Meyer, for soprano, viola and harp (1958), and sketched a motet for baritone and SSA, 'Ye flaming powr's' (1960), from Milton. In 1960 she had set 'All Souls' night' by Frances Cornford and six years later, although ill, she composed three more songs – 'Carrowdore' (St John Irvine), 'O Ghost that has gone' (James Stephens) and 'The mill water' (Edward Thomas) – to make up a set which she called *Looking back*.

Maudlin of Paplewick

Only one more task remained to complete her output: a children's opera, *Maudlin of Paplewick*. Throughout her life, Boyle was attracted to works for the stage. Among her early compositions, she kept the piano score and libretto of an opera, *Undine*, while her mature works included ballets, a masque and a mimed drama. In August 1963, she reported to Sheila Wingfield that she had been writing 'a kind of children's opera' on Ben Jonson's unfinished play 'The Sad Shepherd', of which she had just finished the short score, and had now to orchestrate it.

> There are lovely bits of poetry in it, and it is quite gentle and kindly, not like his bitter plays. One only finds it in a complete edition, so I had never seen it until fairly lately, and as I had always wanted to write an opera, I jumped to it at once, and have not tired of it in the doing.[31]

According to a letter five months later, she was still working on the orchestration, which would take a long time because her eyesight was increasingly susceptible to strain.

> The original is in verse, so I only abridged it for music, and added, where it leaves off, a ballet or pantomime, and a septet of, I hope, sufficiently old words not to go badly with it from 'The King's Quair'. It is very unpretentious, suitable for children, but I always wanted to write an opera, and it is for my own pleasure. I do not propose it as a possible thing to play.[32]

The project was clearly a labour of love, from the first sketch, dated 16 June 1956, to the final mammoth version finished in October 1964. The full score, consisting of 622 pages of manuscript, was bound professionally with the title on the spine in gold lettering. The name of the composer is given in full as 'Ina Boyle', unlike 'I. Boyle' as in many of her manuscripts. Seven preliminary pages include an introductory note on the text and a synopsis of the three acts. The cast list is given together with charming drawings of the eighteen characters and detailed descriptions of the costumes. The chamber orchestra of eleven instruments is also listed. Set in Sherwood Forest, there are two sketches of the stage sets: a woodland scene for Acts I and III and the witch's cottage for Act II. In a matching bound volume of the short score there is one small change in the format. While it contains the same introductory material, the sketches of the characters and the descriptions of the costumes are on the same page.

Even though she realised that the opera would never be performed, it must have brought Boyle tremendous satisfaction to have completed a project that gave her so much enjoyment. It was an impressive physical and mental feat for a woman in her seventies to copy out both the full score and the short score, together with the libretto and copious stage directions. The archaic language of Ben Jonson's text is not altered, but she made one concession to modern taste by giving alternative names which might be used for the shepherds and shepherdesses: Aeglamour (Jonathan or Barnabas), Earine (Anemone or Elizabeth), Mellifleur (Jenifer) and Douce (Jess). The fanciful plot had undertones of the conflict between good and evil, which is resolved in a happy ending. At a time when her health was deteriorating and she was in the closing years of her life, there is no doubt that the work absorbed her creative energies and provided her with an escape into the world of fantasy.

Final years

There were no further public performances of Boyle's orchestral music during her lifetime, but two other works were broadcast by Radio Éireann in the early sixties. In a letter to Sheila Wingfield in 1964, she wrote: 'I had the pleasure of a really beautiful broadcast of some choral hymns I wrote forty years ago.'[33] These were the *Gaelic Hymns* which Vaughan Williams had liked so much when he heard them sung in London by the Oriana Choir. Despite her efforts to promote them, they were rarely performed and this broadcast by the RTÉ Singers, conducted by Dr Hans Waldemar Rosen, was the first time that all five hymns were heard in Ireland.[34] In 1965 her chamber work *Thinke then, my soule* was included in a programme of music by Irish composers in the series 'Masters and Moderns'. The performers were Patrick Ring (tenor), David Lillis (1st violin), Janos Furst (2nd violin), Máire Larchet (viola) and Maurice Meulien (cello).[35]

Boyle's health was failing. In February 1967, she wrote to Elizabeth Maconchy from Bushey Park: 'I have had an X-ray and the result came today. It is cancer and nothing can be done. I want to stay here as long as I can. So far I have no pain, but am very weak.' In spite of the bad news, composing was still on her mind, as she continued: 'I have come upon a most striking old ballad, unknown to me hitherto, called "The Demon Lover". If I can, I will have a shot at setting it for mezzo, baritone, small chorus and orchestra. I have not met anything that so attracted me for ages.'[36] Elizabeth visited her in the nursing home to say goodbye and on 10 March, two days after her seventy-eighth birthday, she died at Castle Clare Nursing Home, Greystones. She is buried in St Patrick's Graveyard, Enniskerry, surrounded by her Crampton and Jephson relatives, and close to her home, Bushey Park.

In 1974 on the publication of Elizabeth Maconchy's tribute, *Ina Boyle: An Appreciation*, the *Irish Times* music critic, Charles Acton, noted that all Boyle's manuscripts were located in TCD Library and proposed some practical ideas to promote her music. He suggested that a television documentary should be made about her with singers Bernadette Greevy and Frank Patterson, that Claddagh Records or the New Irish Recording Company should record her vocal music and that her ballets should be produced by the Cork Ballet Company.

After Boyle's death, there were only a few performances of her music during the remaining years of the twentieth century. In 1977 some of her choral music was featured in two recitals in Monkstown Church by the RTÉ Singers, conducted by Michael Bowles[37] and Eric Sweeney respectively.[38] In his review of the former concert Acton welcomed the rare opportunity of hearing her music:

> I am really grateful for the chance of hearing Ina Boyle's two items. Her distinguished music is so little heard (and was indeed during her life) that every opportunity is important, even though both these are clearly Anglican anthems skilfully and exactly composed for a cathedral choir and organ and not for women's voices. While I found 'The Transfiguration' anthem a bit too long and disjointed the funeral one is a splendid piece in the very best of the tradition of Wesley, Stanford and Vaughan Williams.[39]

In October 2000 the motet *O Thou! Whose Spirit* was performed during the autumn tour of the National Chamber Choir, conducted by Colin Mawby, at concerts in Longford, Belfast, Westmeath and Dublin.[40] According to Martin Adams, who reviewed the final concert in St Stephen's Church, Dublin, 'Her accomplished late-Romantic counterpoint catches the intensity of Henry Vaughan's visionary words.'[41] In October 2013, the six-part motet *The spacious firmament on high* was sung by the cathedral choir at evensong in St Paul's Cathedral, London.

In Belfast, the Ulster Orchestra broadcast two orchestral works on BBC R3: Overture for orchestra in a programme of music by Irish composers on St Patrick's Day 1989, and *The Magic Harp* in 1991. Belfast was also the venue in 2010 for the long-awaited first performance of the violin concerto by the Ulster Orchestra, conducted by Kenneth Montgomery, with Catherine Leonard as soloist. In May 2013, Europe Day was celebrated by concerts in London and Reykjavik, featuring the European Union Youth Orchestra, conducted by Laurent Pillot. The programme consisted of music by Irish composers in honour of Ireland's presidency of the European Union and included Boyle's last orchestral work, *Wildgeese*.

Following the 2010 broadcast on RTÉ Lyric FM of the documentary 'From the Darkness: The life and music of Ina Boyle',[42] there was increased interest in the performance of her music. In 2011 the string quartet and six songs were performed at concerts in Dundalk Institute of Technology, the Hugh Lane

Gallery Dublin and in St Patrick's Church of Ireland, Enniskerry, where her father had served as curate. From October 2013 to April 2014 the score of her Symphony No. 3 was on display at the exhibition 'In Tune: A Millennium of Music in Trinity College Library', and the string quartet was played by the Callino Quartet at a concert of chamber music in the Examination Hall. The quartet also featured in London in April 2016, at an Irish Heritage concert in the Guildhall School of Music and Drama. Meanwhile her songs have been performed at recitals in Wicklow, Dublin, London, Stuttgart and further afield in Australia and China.[43]

In September 2016, the three-week music festival 'Composing the Island: A century of music in Ireland 1916–2016' was held in Dublin. Boyle was represented by three works: the first public performance of Symphony No. 1, 'Glencree', by the RTÉ Concert Orchestra, two settings for tenor and string quartet of poems by John Donne, and the string quartet in E minor. The symphony, which was conducted at the opening concert by Kenneth Montgomery, received a favourable review in the *Irish Examiner*:

> It was the work of Ina Boyle from Wicklow that impressed most ... The harmonic language was colourful. There was refreshing rhythmic energy in parts and assured writing for solo parts, most notably for oboe and cor anglais, well-executed by Concert Orchestra principals. Boyle wrote many works including two more symphonies and an opera. Based on tonight's evidence, her work warrants more than an occasional dust down.[44]

5

A Composer's Life

A thick skin

Ina Boyle was naturally shy and self-effacing, but when it came to her compositions she followed Vaughan Williams' advice to Grace Williams: 'If you're going to be a composer you'll need the hide of a rhinoceros.'[1] Her 'Memoranda' lists the names of numerous conductors – including Adrian Boult, Henry Wood, Dan Godfrey and Landon Ronald – to whom she sent her orchestral scores, only to have them returned. Thanks to the publicity generated for *The Magic Harp*, when it was selected for publication by the Carnegie Trust, the work was performed several times in London and Bournemouth in the 1920s. It remains her only published orchestral work. She continued to send manuscript scores of her other orchestral works to the BBC until the outbreak of war, but none of them was performed.

In 1929 she sent the score of *Phantasy* for violin and chamber orchestra to Sybil Eaton, 'who tried it with Dr Walford Davies but said she could not make it effective'.[2] In 1933 she sent her violin concerto to a succession of violinists including Albert Sammons, Jelly d'Arnanyi (whose secretary returned it unread, saying she had not time to look at it) and Ornea Pernel. Despite these rebuffs, she persevered and sent the work to Adrian Boult at the BBC. It was finally rehearsed on 25 April 1935 by the BBC Orchestra, conducted by Aylmer Buesst with André Mangeot as soloist, but the performance was not broadcast. In January 1944 she sent the score to the leader of the RÉO, Nancie Lord, who gave the Irish premiere of E. J. Moeran's violin concerto in Dublin later that year. She also left orchestral scores with the Radio Éireann librarian for the attention of visiting conductors including Ahn Eik Tai, Ernst Ansermet, Edmond Appia, Jean Martinon and Mosco Carner. But of her three symphonies only one – the *'Glencree'* symphony – was performed, in 1945, at a studio concert conducted by Arthur Duff. Apart from *The Magic Harp, Colin*

Clout, Overture for orchestra and *Wildgeese*, her other orchestral pieces remain unheard.

She circulated her choral works to many distinguished choral conductors – Stanford Robinson, Leslie Woodgate, Herbert Sumsion, David Willcocks, Melville Cook – but only Charles Kennedy Scott featured the *Gaelic Hymns* in concerts by the Oriana Choir. According to her 'Memoranda', she sent copies of her vocal music to singers Harold Bradbury, Steuart Wilson, Joan Elwes and Sophie Wyss. In Dublin she gave copies of songs to 'Mr T. O'Sullivan' (Tomás Ó Súilleabháin) and Jean Nolan, both active broadcasters at that time. Her efforts to have her chamber music performed were more successful, particularly through the Macnaghten concerts. But although her string quartet was recorded by the Macnaghten Quartet it was not played subsequently in public. Back in Ireland she gave the score to Nancie Lord for the Cuala Quartet and later lent the original score to Olive Zorian, founder of the Zorian Quartet, when she visited Bushey Park, but no performance ensued.

Throughout her life, Boyle realised the importance of having her works published, but her publications represent only a small proportion of her overall output. In 1922 *The Magic Harp* was published by Stainer & Bell for the Carnegie Trust, but despite her best efforts none of her other orchestral works were published. She paid for the publication of several choral works: 'He will swallow up death' (1915), 'Wilt not Thou O Lord' (1915), *Soldiers at Peace* (1917) and *The Transfiguration* (1923). Stainer & Bell published 'A song of enchantment' (1923) and 'A song of shadows' (1926), but refused other vocal music until 1935, when they accepted *A Spanish Pastoral*.

She obtained estimates for the publication of the *Gaelic Hymns* from Stainer & Bell and from J & W Chester, who finally published five *Gaelic Hymns* in 1930 and insisted on keeping the copyright. Despite having an introduction from Vaughan Williams to Hubert Foss, music editor of OUP, none of the songs or choral music that she sent him were accepted for publication until 1939, when she paid the cost of publication herself for the chamber work *Thinke then, my soule* (1938). In 1943 OUP published her arrangement of a song by Purcell, 'With sick and famished eyes'.

Her early success with *The Magic Harp* encouraged Boyle to enter other works for the Carnegie Trust Scheme and the Patron's Fund. She regularly sent scores to the selection committee for the International Festival for Contemporary Music, which provided a platform for so many living composers, only to have them rejected. This constant rejection did not deter her from entering competitions and she sent scores for consideration to the Civil Service Choir and the *Daily Telegraph* competitions, the Three Choirs

Festival and the Edinburgh Festival Society. Despite the selection of *Lament for Bion* for 'Honourable Mention' and a Diploma in the Music category of the Olympic Art Competition in 1948, the work was never performed. Boyle received some unaccustomed publicity in Dublin when the awards were presented to three Irish winners by the President of the Irish Olympic Council, Colonel Eamon Broy, at a ceremony in the Royal Hibernian Academy of Arts.[3] The other recipients were the artist Letitia Hamilton, for her painting 'Meath Point-to-Point', and the writer Stanislaus Lynch, for his prose piece 'Echoes of the Hunting Horn'. In making the presentations, Colonel Broy said that Ireland should begin preparing for the next Olympic Games in 1952.[4]

Family duties

Vaughan Williams had commended Boyle for her courage 'in going on with so little recognition'. Although the prospect of recognition faded, her compulsion to compose for her own pleasure did not diminish. In 1963 she wrote: 'I love this dear house so much that I never mind about lack of musical success, though of course it would have been very welcome, and as long as I can stay here I am well content.'[5] Her choice to live all her life in seclusion at Bushey Park was dictated by family circumstances. From her mother's death in 1932, when Boyle was forty-three, she cared for both her younger sister Phyllis, who died six years later, and for her father, who lived until 1951.[6] As time went on she became fully responsible for the running of the house and the estate and for the welfare of the employees.[7] She kept cows and hens and made her own butter and jam. On hearing that 'one could make a profit out of them' she grew a crop of peas. The harvesting machine was unable to negotiate the entrance gate, so that a wall had to be demolished and rebuilt afterwards, which used up all the profit.[8]

Although she read widely and listened to the BBC Third Programme, she was cut off from the world outside. Apart from her visits to London, she had few opportunities of hearing live music or of making the kind of contacts that would enable her music to be heard. The intervention of the war was another factor that prevented her from gaining recognition. By the time it was over she was a middle-aged woman from another era. She was a member of the MAI from its inception in 1948 to 1964 but, unlike her contemporaries, she did not attend meetings or become a member of the Council. In 1954 when the Composers' Group organised a series of lunchtime concerts of music by Irish composers at TCD, she was not represented.[9]

After her father's death she lived on in Bushey Park for sixteen years. She enjoyed occasional visits from her relatives and her London friends. Elizabeth Maconchy's daughters, Nicola LeFanu and Anna Dunlop, have vivid memories of visiting Bushey Park with their mother and of drinking brown-coloured water from the spring opposite the front door.[10] When Anne Macnaghten, Arnold Ashby and Elizabeth Maconchy visited in April 1955, Boyle said it was the happiest week of her life. She invited the MAI Composers' Group to Bushey Park for a recital by the Macnaghten String Quartet of music by Vaughan Williams, Purcell, Bloch and Maconchy.[11] Seóirse Bodley, who was present, remembers being offered a choice of Indian or China tea.

Sheila Wingfield regretted that she was unable to attend and admonished her for not including any of her own works in the programme: 'I do call this shockingly reprehensible. You are invariably over-modest but this I do honestly think is altogether too humble of you.'[12] In her memoir, *Sun Too Fast*, published after Boyle's death, Sheila gives a sympathetic and colourful account of Ina Boyle, 'who lived the sad, full, solitary, humorous life of a saint', and the household at Bushey Park.[13] They shared a mutual interest in the creative process and corresponded over the years. In 1938 Boyle wrote an appreciative letter of thanks for an inscribed copy of Sheila's first book of poetry: 'Though I know nothing technically about poetry I feel the forms of them always satisfying and distinguished, and they have a clarity and spareness that I greatly like, and that reminds me sometimes of things in the Greek Anthology.'[14]

In a letter twenty years later she referred to some recent poems that Sheila had written despite her health problems: 'It is plucky of you to write in the face of such pain and difficulty, but there is no sign of it in them and I know that you, like me, believe that it is not when one is most at ease and well that the best work comes.'[15] Sheila's departure from Powerscourt House to live abroad left a void in Boyle's life:

> It utterly surprised me that anything I ever said or did should have influenced you in any way – it was all the other way around I thought, and I often find myself wondering what you would have thought of this or that, and of the many interesting things you told me about people and books etc. It was like a light gone out when you went away from here and I know my father loved your visits and talks with him too.[16]

In 1963 Boyle presented a silver challenge cup, in memory of her father, to the Powerscourt Ploughing Society for competition at the annual ploughing match, which was held that year in Bushey Park.[17] The upkeep of the old house remained a priority. Three years before her death she wrote that she had 'the most unexpected good fortune to have shares in a take-over bid', and kept some of the cash part of the payment to do some urgent repairs:

> I got new stair carpets and curtains and had the roof repaired and some of the rooms re-distempered, all as near the old ones as I could so there is no outward change. I don't find growing old changes my likes and dislikes at all.[18]

She depended more than ever on her wireless, and bought a tape recorder 'to try and trap good broadcasts, but at present it just twirls round and round till I learn its ways'.[19] She also bought a television set. During the last two years of her life, prompted by enquiries from America by genealogist Basil O'Connell, she developed a keen interest in the Jephson side of her family. She preserved the letters in a folder labelled 'Keep carefully. Correspondence with Mr Basil O'Connell, the genealogist, about the Jephson family arising out of Brigadier Maurice Jephson's book *An Anglo-Irish Miscellany*. Mr O'Connell helped to supplement and correct many pedigrees etc. in that very interesting book, especially the branch of Carrick-on-Suir Jephsons to which I belong.' The folder also contains letters from her cousins Catherine Wood and Adelaide Hutchins, who sent her further information about the family tree.[20] She had made arrangements for letters from Thomas Moore, Sir Walter Scott and Maria Edgeworth to her great grandfather Sir Philip Crampton to be preserved as he had wished, but left instructions in her will that all her letters from her mother and sister were to be burned unread. She wished to be remembered only for her compositions.

A forgotten legacy

If during her life her compositions were her priority, after her death her musical legacy remains intact. Elizabeth Maconchy, her 'musical executor', and Brian Boydell, then professor of music at the University of Dublin, made arrangements that her manuscripts and scores, which were donated by her cousin Doreen Boyle, would be housed in the Manuscripts Library of Trinity College Dublin. There they were catalogued by Síle Ní Thiarnaigh, Music Librarian. In addition to the Crampton papers, the collection includes her 'Memoranda', family photographs, newspaper cuttings and 'A few notes on Lessons from Dr Vaughan Williams'. Copies of her published works are also to be found in the British Library, the Bodleian Library, Oxford, the BBC Music Library, Cumann Náisiúnta na gCor and the Contemporary Music Centre, Dublin.

Ina Boyle was not the only Irish woman composer of her time whose music has been forgotten,[21] but she was certainly the most prolific. Over sixty years she produced a steady stream of compositions in the principal musical genres, excluding solo piano music. The sheer volume of her output reflects her lifelong ambition to be taken seriously as a composer. Her manuscripts are carefully written and dated, some are hand-sewn in cardboard folders, others are professionally bound. Copies of full scores and parts of her most substantial orchestral works comprise hundreds of manuscript pages, with revisions noted in the margins.

The texts of her choral and vocal works are also handwritten, and the title pages are often decorated with ornate script and sketches. Details of performances are sometimes given, and the scores of her stage and ballet works contain stage directions, background notes and watercolour sketches of costumes and scenery. Many of her orchestral works are prefaced by quotations, while the alternative text that she wrote for her symphony no. 3, *In the Darkness*, is painstakingly copied into the score. She was clearly inspired by poetry and literature, ranging from Greek mythology and medieval texts through Elizabethan, Victorian and Anglo-Irish authors to contemporary poets. Her love of nature was stimulated by the beauty of the landscape and the passing of the seasons over the Wicklow mountains and lakes. But her choice of archaic and funereal themes for many of her later works was out of tune with modern times. It is also likely that the large forces required for the performance of her symphonies and stage works mitigated against their performance, particularly in Dublin. One of Boyle's contemporaries, Frederick May, identified the lack of a good music-publishing firm in Ireland as one of the serious shortcomings affecting Irish composers.[22] Certainly, the fact that so little of her music was published contributed to its neglect by performers. It is notable that the style of her music changed very little over the years. In 1963 she wrote: 'I must say I see very little I like these days, either in painting or poetry and some modern music seems sheer nonsense.'[23] She remained uninfluenced by contemporary European developments and maintained her own individual voice throughout. According to Elizabeth Maconchy:

> Her music is predominately quiet and serious, never brilliant, though it has its moments of wit or passion. In idiom it is closest perhaps to Vaughan Williams in his early middle period – but it is not just a pale

reflection of his style; her music always speaks with a personal tone of voice, which at its best can express deep feeling by simple means.[24]

The composer Michael Tippett, who was a student at the Royal College of Music at that time, deliberately avoided taking lessons with Vaughan Williams as he felt that his pupils 'simply wrote feeble, watered down V.W'.[25] But this was by no means the case with other students of Vaughan Williams, such as Elizabeth Maconchy herself, who had broadened her horizons with European study and had discovered the music of Bartok. In 1931, in fact, Vaughan Williams had suggested to Boyle that she should study abroad but, unable to escape from her family commitments, she missed such opportunities. Unlike some of her contemporaries, she did not belong to the 'Celtic Twilight' school of Irish composers either, her late romanticism lacking nationalist leanings. She was more engaged by the challenges of form and colour in everything she wrote.

In revisiting the life and work of Ina Boyle it is appropriate to consider whether it is time to bring her music back from oblivion. Her substantial archive of manuscripts and her published music await rediscovery and performance. Despite disappointment and constant rejection, which she endured without complaint, she never deviated from her chosen path as a composer. It is hoped that this publication will add impetus to the revival of interest in her works, and that her music will be heard not as museum pieces, but as the compositions of a remarkable Irish woman composer who deserves to be remembered.

The Music of Ina Boyle
An Essay by Séamas de Barra

Much of the student work that Ina Boyle produced under the supervision of her distinguished composition teachers – who included Charles Wood, Percy Buck and C. H. Kitson – is preserved amongst her papers in Trinity College Dublin. It attests to a thorough and extensive training and it ranges from the standard drill in harmony and counterpoint to more elaborate exercises in the composition of short instrumental pieces, the setting of texts for voice and piano or for choir, formal analysis and orchestration. Her creative gifts developed quite naturally in tandem with these technical studies and emerged in an easy, unforced way. The line between an assigned task and a genuine composition may have been blurred initially, but by the outbreak of the Great War in 1914, when she was twenty-five years old, some of the pieces she had written seemed to her to be something more than mere exercises: these included over twenty songs, a handful of choral pieces, an *Elegy* for violoncello and orchestra, and a work for baritone solo, chorus and orchestra entitled *Ireland*, to words by Walt Whitman.[1] She scored a modest success in 1913 when both the *Elegy* and one of the songs were awarded prizes at Sligo Feis Ceoil,[2] and encouraged by this, perhaps, in 1915 she wrote two anthems to texts that seemed appropriate for a time of war, and had them published in London at her own expense.

From then until the mid-1960s, a few years before she died, Ina Boyle produced a steady stream of compositions in virtually all genres: orchestral music, chamber music, choral music, vocal music and even, at the end of her life, opera. Despite this productivity, however, much of what she wrote – including some of her finest work – remained unheard at the time it was written and still awaits performance today. There were a few periods in her life when her music did succeed to some extent in reaching the public, particularly in the 1920s and the 1940s, but, on the whole, performances remained intermittent and wider recognition eluded her altogether.

Both her retiring temperament and the circumstances of her personal life, as described in the first part of this book, partially explain this neglect. But it must also be remembered that in the early decades of the twentieth century, the period of Boyle's most intense creative activity, musical life in Ireland was very underdeveloped, and consequently not particularly conducive to the fostering and promotion of native compositional talent.[3] The occasional performances her music received in Dublin and in Cork were probably more or less on a par with those enjoyed by her Irish contemporaries. Her natural inclination was to look to England, and particularly to London, as a more promising arena, especially in the 1920s when there were very few opportunities for her work to be heard at home. Her one significant success there, however, did not lead to anything further and she never secured a lasting foothold on the English musical scene. Her approach to composing was very unbusinesslike; rarely in advance of putting pen to paper does she seem to have inquired what kind of composition might best stand a chance of gaining a hearing. The systematic identification of existing or likely performance opportunities and of tailoring her work accordingly was not really part of her thinking, and this led to the expenditure of a great deal of energy on the creation of scores, often quite substantial scores, in which – and not for the want of trying – she subsequently failed to arouse any interest.

The object of the present essay is to survey this largely unknown corpus of work by one of the most elusive and intriguing figures in early twentieth-century Irish music. Its aim is not to be exhaustive, but rather – by focusing on selected works – to give an idea of her technical and stylistic approach to composition and to show the range of her achievement. If it succeeds in illuminating to some degree the nature of Ina Boyle's art and leads to a deeper appreciation of her position in the history of Irish music, it will have realised its purpose, but it is also hoped that it may prompt others to examine her work for themselves and, perhaps, help redeem half a century of neglect by stimulating the interest of prospective performers.

Having stretched her wings with the composition of *Ireland* in 1914, Ina Boyle attempted another work for mixed-voice chorus and orchestra in 1916. In the issue of the *Spectator* for 13 May that year she came across 'Soldiers at Peace', a poem by Herbert Asquith,[4] who at the time was serving as an officer in the British army. Boyle was clearly moved by the meditation on those who had fallen in the war – 'whose still unfaded spring / Is graven deep in England's memory' – and she completed the work quickly: the manuscript full score is dated 'Summer 1916'. When, the following year, the Carnegie United Kingdom Trust established a scheme for the publication of music by British composers,[5]

Boyle submitted *Soldiers at Peace* for consideration and, although it was not listed amongst the successful works, it was warmly commended by the reading panel. She herself thought sufficiently highly of it to have the vocal score published at her own expense by Novello & Co. in the same year, 1917, but, despite the topicality of the subject, this does not appear to have led to any performances.[6] Technically, *Soldiers at Peace* marks a considerable advance on the earlier Whitman setting and it shows far greater confidence in the handling of both voices and orchestra. As befits the theme, the work inhabits a similar stylistic world to that of the dignified, *nobilmente* choral writing of senior British contemporaries – Parry comes to mind – and the harmonic idiom, with its pervasive chromatic third-related harmonies, its diminished seventh chords and its augmented sixths, carries faint echoes of the Wagner of *Lohengrin*. The overall effect is somewhat weakened by an excessive reliance on third-related progressions – the E flat major-G major-B major succession of the opening bars being typical – which, while undoubtedly colourful, tend to be effective in inverse proportion to their use. The result here is a tonal indecisiveness that makes a sense of purposeful forward movement difficult to achieve over any length of time. This may not be music that reveals any notably original creative personality, but it is an interesting work nonetheless, as it clearly reflects the efforts of the emerging composer to take the standard procedures learned by the erstwhile student and to develop them into something more personal. The conspicuous avoidance of obvious dominant-tonic relationships in the harmony, for example, indicates a desire to transcend the schoolroom, but it also suggests that the inclination towards a modal idiom – which was soon to come to the fore quite clearly – was latent in Boyle's style long before she commenced lessons with Vaughan Williams, who might otherwise be regarded as the decisive influence in this regard.

In 1918, the Carnegie Trust committee rejected her setting of Julia Ward Howe's 'Battle Hymn of the Republic', also for mixed-voice chorus and full orchestra (this time with the addition of solo soprano). It was a curious choice of text on Boyle's part. Howe's well-known words (which were first published in 1862) are so indissolubly associated with 'John Brown's Body', the anonymous popular song of the American Civil War – the *Hymn* was in fact specially written to be sung to the tune – that any other music, no matter how well composed, is destined to seem oddly incongruous. Boyle's score does not allude to the traditional melody, and there is not the slightest indication that she was even aware of its existence. The setting, which in itself is dramatically conceived and often effectively realised, is serenely oblivious to this glaring absence against which the work's every thematic idea and every compositional gesture will inevitably be heard. Boyle composed a number of other works for chorus and orchestra at well-spaced intervals until the early 1940s, but apart from *Soldiers at Peace*, which was sung in 1920, none of them has been performed.[7]

The following year, she completed her first purely orchestral works: *A Sea Poem*, the manuscript of which is dated January, and *The Magic Harp: Rhapsody for Orchestra*, dated March–November 1919. Again, she submitted both scores for consideration by the Carnegie Trust selection committee, and while *A Sea Poem* merely elicited encouraging remarks in 1919, *The Magic Harp* fared better in 1920 and was included amongst the works chosen for publication.

One wonders why *The Magic Harp* rather than *A Sea Poem* was selected, because in many respects the latter is a more accomplished score. Tonally, it hovers ambiguously between E minor and its modal variants and accordingly marks a decisive move towards the composer's characteristic modally inflected harmonic language. The work is designed as a theme (preceded by an introduction), six variations and a finale. The structure of the theme itself is a matter of some technical interest. Marked *Lento*, it commences with an eight-bar period (internally organised as 2+2+4 bars). This is immediately repeated with the final bars adapted to lead to a central, contrasting five-bar phrase (2+3), and the theme is then rounded off with a modified return of the initial period, now supplied with a new consequent phrase and supplemented by a related additional four bars (2+2+4+4). This clear-cut design means that the underlying structure of the theme remains easily identifiable in each of the succeeding variations, however texturally reconstituted it may be. Furthermore, the harmonic articulation is so distinctive that modifications to the basic phrase structure – whether by means of phrase extension, expansion or other kinds of internal remodelling – never obscure its fundamental character.

Another point of interest is the manner in which the variations themselves are organised. The theme, which is left open on the dominant chord (B major), is followed by three linked variations: (i) *Più animato*, (ii) *Più vivace, scherzando* and (iii) *Più largamente*. The first two of these adhere to the structure of the theme exactly, while the third variation is subject both to subtle modification and a considerable expansion of the final phrase before closing on the tonic. Not only is this approach successful in avoiding undue predictability, but the expansion of the third gives the three variations together an overall sense of culmination and, in conjunction with the tonal closure, creates the feeling that they constitute a self-contained section – almost a movement – within the larger structure. The next variation (iv) is, in contrast, an *Adagio, molto tranquillo* and might be considered to occupy the place of a slow movement, a sense that the shift of the tonal centre to C reinforces. It is linked to the final two variations, (v) *Allegro molto* and (vi) *Più mosso*, which are themselves also linked. Although the fast tempo of these two variations provides a vital contrast to the earlier part of the work, they create no sense of an ending, partly because Boyle again shifts the tonal centre in variation (vi), this time to a quasi-modal B minor. It is left to the finale proper, *Lento, quasi tempo I°*, to restore the tonic, and with references both to the material of the introduction and to the original version of the theme, to bring the work to a quiet conclusion.

The handling of variation technique, as well as the way in which the individual variations are welded into a single movement that encompasses both internal contrast and a satisfying overall coherence, undoubtedly makes *A Sea Poem* one of the finest of Ina Boyle's early works. But while *A Sea Poem* has never been performed, *The Magic Harp*, which is far less impressive from the point of view of compositional technique, has become one of her best-known pieces. The adjudicators for the Carnegie Trust may well have been attracted to it by the greater piquancy and memorability of the thematic material – *A Sea Poem* is less distinguished in this regard – as well as by the appeal of the programme and its allusions, however vague, to ancient Irish legend.

In order to explain the title and elucidate the poetic theme of *The Magic Harp*, Ina Boyle supplied a note for inclusion in the score:

> The Durd-Alba (the wind among the apple trees) was the magical harp of the ancient gods of Ireland. It had three strings – the iron string of sleep, the bronze string of laughter, and the silver string, the sound of which made all men weep. These three strings were also supposed to evoke the three seasons into which the year was then divided.

This paragraph is taken from *Unseen Kings*, a volume comprising a play and a handful of poems published by Eva Gore-Booth (1870–1926) in 1904, where it appears as a footnote to 'The Harper's Song of the Seasons'.[8] (There are several discrepancies between Gore-Booth's text and Boyle's reproduction, however, including the name of the harp, which should read 'Durd-*abla*', not 'Durd-*Alba*'.)[9] Boyle had come across 'The Harper's Song of Seasons' and even sketched a setting of it for voice and piano when she was still a young girl, and although the song never appears to have been completed, the poem clearly lingered in her imagination.[10] While it is not reproduced or even alluded to in the published score, it seems that she considered it relevant also to *The Magic Harp*, and a handwritten copy is to be found with the MS. Interestingly, the order in which the three strings of the harp are listed in the note – iron (sleep), bronze (laughter) and silver (weeping) – is reversed in the poem, and this reversed order corresponds more closely to the character of the successive sections of the rhapsody. The idea of the three-stringed harp is also personalised in the poem in a way not suggested by the note and this, too, seems to illuminate the emotional import of Boyle's music:

> The wind that blows among the apple-trees
> Of my desire, breaks through the world's control,
> And shakes with many secret melodies
> The silver harp-string twisted round my soul ...

The instrument in question appears to be the harp of the Dagda (or Daghdha) who was the principal figure among the mythological Tuatha Dé Danann, the ancient god-like race of Ireland. It is referred to towards the close of the saga, *The Second Battle of Moytura*, when the Dagda retrieves it from the Fomorians who carried it off at the end of the battle. Both Whitley Stokes, who published his translation of the saga in 1891, and Lady Gregory in her *Gods and Fighting Men* of 1904, tell how the harp had several names, one of which was Dur-da-Bla (of which 'Durd-abla' is a garbled variant), meaning 'oak of two (greens)' (Stokes) or 'Oak of two Blossoms' (Gregory). The source of Eva Gore-Booth's information is not known, but 'the wind among the apple-trees' appears to be a somewhat fanciful translation.

Ex. 1: *The Magic Harp*, bars 1–6

The Magic Harp commences with a vivid, arresting motif that immediately establishes the legendary atmosphere of the rhapsody (Ex. 1). Although the twenty-five-bar introductory paragraph into which it is extended adumbrates several of the themes heard later in the work, it is a little too fragmented and aimless to be completely convincing. Boyle further accentuates its weakness by bringing it to a complete stop, separating it from the ensuing section by a full bar's rest. Sparingly used, such rhetorical breaks have their place, but if resorted to more frequently, as they tend to be in *The Magic Harp*, not only does the constant interruption of the flow of the music become wearisome, it also loosens the structure of the composition. The main body of the work falls into three principal parts and (following the poem) these may be taken to represent in turn the season of spring and the silver string of sorrow; the season of summer and the bronze string of laughter; and the season of winter and the iron string of sleep. As at the end of the introduction, however, each part – which is characterised by its own distinct thematic material – is clearly demarcated from the others either by a pause or by a rest. For all the undeniable attractiveness of the ideas, therefore, the overall impression the score makes is one of excessive sectionality and short-windedness. This tendency to fragmentation is only further emphasised by the fairly obvious internal subdivision of each of the constituent sections, as shown in the diagram below.

INTRODUCTION	A	B		C	CODA
	a–b–a¹	c–d–c¹	[INTRO.]	e–e¹	[INTRO.]

Ex. 2: *The Magic Harp*, bars 26–37

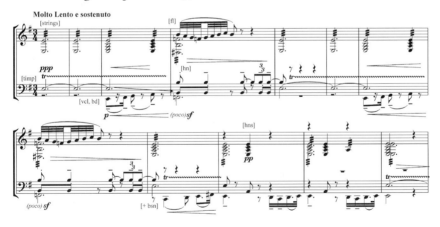

The initial theme of the A/a section (*Molto Lento e sostenuto*) consists of a dark, brooding idea in the bass supplemented by a swirling motif in the woodwind (Ex. 2). It is immediately repeated in a varied form and leads to the central sub-section (A/b) in which a delicate, graceful fragment of melody in the woodwind acquires a touching poignancy from the mournful, chromatic motif that underpins it in the strings (Ex. 3). The whole passage strongly recalls the following lines from the poem:

> The wind that blows among the apple-trees
> Is as a harp of sorrow in the spring,
> Piercing the sunshine of sweet melodies
> With the sharp crying of the silver string –

Ex. 3: *The Magic Harp*, bars 52–57

An abbreviated version of the opening idea returns and, after a pause, the tempo picks up for a modulatory transition to the B section that anticipates its principal theme, a breezy tune (*Allegro, ma non troppo*) on the first violins offset by a flowing semiquaver accompaniment in the violas (Ex. 4). Skilfully developed into the first significant climax of the work, this idea is succeeded by a quieter central episode in which short, fanfare-like phrases are tossed between

Ex. 4: *The Magic Harp*, bars 92–97

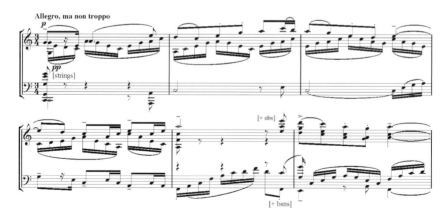

solo horn and individual woodwind instruments against a background of sustained string harmonies and rippling harp figuration. The brief resumption of the main *allegro* idea culminates in a return of the initial motif of the introduction, which has now acquired a motto-like function in helping to bind together the rhapsody's disparate thematic content.

The C section (*Adagio, non troppo*) follows immediately. Unlike the previous two sections, each of which was a miniature three-part structure in itself, this final section is in two parts. A new group of ideas (C/e) commences with a theme on the first violins (Ex. 5), which may be intended to depict the 'iron sleep for the world's ease, / When the leaves fall and every bough is bare'. The music becomes increasingly more urgent and it culminates in a climax of considerable intensity that represents the emotional high-point of the work. A brief, varied restatement of the main ideas (C/e^1) is followed by a short coda in which the motto-like motif of the introduction is heard one last time, bringing the rhapsody to a close with a final invocation of the world of legend that inspired it.

Ex. 5: *The Magic Harp*, bars 159–163

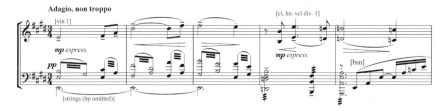

Although the publication of *The Magic Harp* must at the time have seemed a promising portent for the future, Ina Boyle never succeeded in having another of her orchestral scores published and, as has already been mentioned, many of them remained unperformed. This was not the case with her next orchestral piece, however. *Colin Clout*, subtitled 'A Pastoral after Spenser's *Shepheard's Calender*', is not only one of her most attractive shorter orchestral works, but is also perhaps the first in which her characteristic modal idiom emerges with assured consistency. In 1922, the year after it was completed, it was performed at the Royal College of Music in London by the London Symphony Orchestra, conducted by Adrian Boult, and it was heard again twice during the 1930s and twice more during the 1940s. A subtler score in many respects than *The Magic Harp*, it nonetheless retains the appeal of the earlier work while at the same time showing far greater technical sophistication both in its formal organisation and in the way the thematic material is handled.

Edmund Spenser's *The Shepheardes Calender* (1579) consists of twelve 'aeglogues' (eclogues), one for each month of the year. Boyle's work is based on the first of these, 'Januarie', which concerns itself with the plight of the lovelorn shepherd boy, Colin Clout. This personage appears in a number of Spenser's poems and seems to have been intended to represent the poet himself: apart from *The Shepheardes Calender*, he also features in *Colin Clouts Come Home Againe* (1595) and even makes an appearance in Book VI (1596) of *The Faerie Queen*.[11] Boyle copied the entire first 'aeglogue' into her manuscript as a preface to the score, but she gave no indication that the music was intended to be anything other than the most generalised reflection of its contents. Indeed Spenser's eclogue itself is essentially a mood piece in which very little happens: the first nine of its thirteen stanzas tell how Colin leads his flock to the hills and laments his lovelorn state, observing how the inclement winter weather mirrors his sorry plight; the tenth stanza introduces his friend Hobbinol, who attempts in vain to distract him; and the final three stanzas lead the poem to its crisis as Colin complains that his music has lost the power to ease his tormented soul and breaks his shepherd's pipe in a fit of despair. As a general scenario, this is perfectly suited to musical treatment and it is possible to detect a comparable emotional contour in Boyle's work.

Ex. 6: *Colin Clout*, bars 1–9

Colin Clout commences with a short unaccompanied solo for the flute, the instrument the composer uses to represent the shepherd lad throughout the piece. This idea, together with an answering phrase in the full orchestra (Ex. 6), forms the basis of a twenty-nine-bar introductory section that in a few deft strokes suggests the woebegone boy's sad piping and creates the mood of gentle melancholy that permeates the music. A greatly expanded and intensified version of this opening paragraph returns at the end and so may be considered to frame a larger, composite central section consisting of two main subdivisions, thus giving the work the overall form A-B/C-A^1, although the different sections are not self-contained and there is much thematic cross-referencing.

Ex. 7: *Colin Clout*, bars 30–38

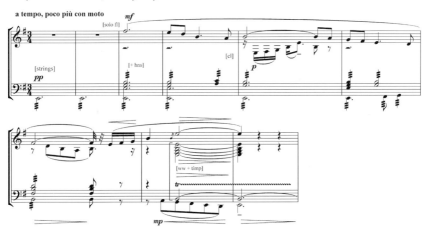

The tempo picks up a little for the B section (*Poco più con moto*) and two new ideas are heard: the first continues to feature the solo flute (Ex. 7), and the second (marked *Più adagio*) introduces an important stately idea on the strings (Ex. 8). This has an ardent, pleading quality about it and one may hear in it, perhaps, an evocation of Colin's despairing cry to the Gods:

Ex. 8: *Colin Clout*, bars 50–53

> Ye Gods of love, that pitie lovers payne,
> (If any Gods the paine of lovers pitie)
> Looke from above, where you in joyes remain,
> And bowe your eares unto my dolefull dittie

With fleeting allusions to the themes of the introduction, these ideas are developed into a climax, after which the music breaks off and the tonality changes from the prevailing Aeolian E minor, to E major for the C section. Once again, the tempo picks up a little (*Poco più mosso*) and two further new ideas serve to lighten the mood and introduce a more carefree atmosphere (marked *a* and *b* in Ex. 9). Clearly, Hobbinol has arrived on the scene with his well-meant but futile attempt to cheer up Colin:

> His clownish gifts and curtesies I disdaine,
> His kiddes, his cracknelles, and his early fruit.
> Ah, foolish Hobbinol! Thy gyfts be vayne;
> Colin them gives to Rosalind againe.

Ex. 9: *Colin Clout*, bars 82–89

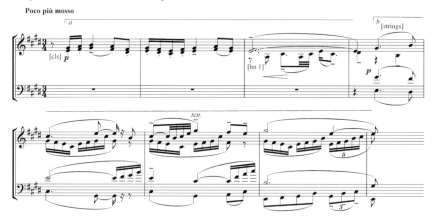

But the lighter mood does not last long and the music rises to a second and more powerful climax that graphically depicts the heart-broken Colin's rejection of Hobbinol's friendly overtures. The atmosphere remains uneasy as the opening ideas return for the A[1] section, and the music becomes increasingly agitated as Colin's despair deepens. Not only has Rosalind (the beloved) belittled his art – 'Shee deignes not my good will, but doth reprove, / And of my rural musicke holdeth scorne' – but he finds that it is no longer a comfort even to himself. Boyle depicts the crisis, the destruction of his instrument – 'So broke his oaten pype' – very simply but effectively with two abrupt *fortissimo* chords, twice sounded, on the lower woodwind and brass. After that, the music ebbs away, fading out on a low-pitched, *pianissimo* E minor chord.

Although Boyle had long nurtured the ambition to write a symphony, the completion of her first essay in the genre proved to be a fairly protracted process and the work gradually took shape between 1924 and 1927 under the watchful eye of Vaughan Williams, with whom she had commenced lessons in 1923.[12] It is conceived as a piece of nature music that sets out to evoke a specific landscape. On the manuscript score, 'Symphony for Orchestra' appears as a descriptive subtitle while, tellingly, the principal title of the work is *'Glencree' (In the Wicklow Hills)*. The whole centre of County Wicklow on the east coast of Ireland is mountainous upland. The Glencree referred to in the title of the symphony is a picturesque valley towards the northern end of the county, and at the eastern end of this valley lies Enniskerry, Ina Boyle's native village. She loved this countryside deeply and it undoubtedly elicited from her a strong imaginative response.

Curiously, such depictions of the countryside are not commonly found in the work of Irish composers. Even those who consciously set out to create a distinctive Irish art music in the early decades of the twentieth century by and large tended to overlook the country's landscape as a possible source of inspiration. This topographical approach, whether urban or pastoral, seems to have been much more congenial to contemporary English composers, and it is difficult to think of many Irish equivalents of Vaughan Williams' evocations of Norfolk, the Fen Country or even London, Herbert Howells' of Gloucestershire, Gustav Holst's of Somerset and the Cotswolds, and so on. One recalls *Meath Pastoral* (1940) by Arthur Duff, perhaps, and *In Glenade* (1942) by Joan Trimble, both for string orchestra, and Seán Ó Riada's pastoral elegy *The Banks of Sullane* (1956). Very little else comes to mind. But if *'Glencree' (In the Wicklow Hills)* is, therefore, a somewhat unusual work in the Irish context, it is also atypical of Ina Boyle's own work, the background to which is more usually of a literary nature. As Elizabeth Maconchy pointed out: 'Ina's inspiration almost always came from poetry: even her purely instrumental works were usually headed by a quotation, a few lines perhaps, which had set off a train of thought and fired her musical imagination.'[13]

The quotations with which Boyle liked to preface her scores are not merely indications of the sources of her inspiration, however, as Maconchy suggests; they are also intended to create in the listener a frame of mind sympathetic to the reception of her music. In seeking to indicate what she wished her *'Glencree'* symphony to convey, she chose two extracts that are particularly apt epitomes of its mood and atmosphere. The first is an excerpt from *In Search of Ireland* by H. V. Morton, a well-known and prolific English travel writer of the period (Boyle clearly appended this extract retrospectively as the book was not published until 1930, a few years after the symphony was completed). It is an evocative and lyrical description of the Wicklow Mountains:

> The great hills, more savage even than Dartmoor, lie fold on fold, some long and gentle in outline, some sharp and conical; and in their hollows you come unexpectedly to deep lakes, such as Lough Dan, lying like a patch of fallen sky. Little brown streams trickle through the peat. The whole landscape is a study in various browns; brown peat like dark chocolate; black brown water; light brown grass; dark brown pyramids of cut peat stacked at intervals along the brown road.
>
> But in the evening the hills turn blue. White mists rise in the hollows and lie there like thin veils hung from hill to hill. The sun sets. And there is no sound but the wind blowing through the tough grass and the thin trickle of water running to the valleys.[14]

To amplify this, Boyle has added a few lines by Joseph Campbell, the Belfast-born poet who had settled in County Wicklow by 1915, and who eventually, in 1921, bought a small farm in Lackandaragh in Glencree, about four miles west of Enniskerry:

> The black and twisted trees
> The delicate web of blue
> That veils the hills,
> The brown water that spills
> Over the rock,
> The grey burial stones,
> The green and springing wood ...[15]

Both of these extracts are notable for their muted palette of colours: various shades of brown that mingle and merge, blue, grey, green and white. There is nothing startling here, nothing garish, nothing brash; these are the soft tones of the Wicklow countryside, tending a little towards bleakness at times, perhaps, but restful, too, in their very uneventfulness. It is less in bold contrasts that the attraction of this landscape is to be found – although it has its dramatic aspects – than in its undulating contours and subtle variations of hue. For

Boyle (as, indeed, for her neighbour, Joseph Campbell), it is a landscape that seems to have been imbued with an almost mystical intensity; it nourished her imagination, and she attempted to communicate its strong emotional impact in her music. She was remarkably successful in finding the means to do this and her naturally unassertive manner is particularly suited to reflect the gentler features of the landscape. But the scenery also encompasses grandeur, and the environment can be grimly inhospitable as well as welcoming, and these very different moods are not ignored in the music. The lasting impression the symphony makes, however, is one of peace, of tranquillity (it is interesting to note how often Boyle has recourse to *tranquillo* as a musical direction) and of an almost impersonal sense of contemplation, although the whole is also shot through with a sadness that brings to mind 'A lost voice / In lonely fields', as Joseph Campbell memorably put it.[16]

The symphony is designed in three movements. This is not in itself noteworthy: since César Franck established a popular and viable model in his Symphony in D minor (1886–88) it became a fairly common alternative to the established four-movement form, especially with composers who no longer either desired or felt the need to include a lighter dance-derived movement or scherzo. With the slow (or slower) movement now occupying the central position between two fast (or faster) outer movements, the overall architectural balance of the symphony was still felt to be satisfactory. For Boyle, however, whose music was predominantly meditative in character, it was not an ideal approach: neither the weighty, developmental sonata *allegro* nor the high-spirited rondo finale was of much use to her. In her own quiet way, she determined on a fairly novel modification of the ground plan: she reversed the expected pattern and placed a single fast movement between two slow outer movements. Ending a symphony with a slow movement was not, of course, without distinguished precedent – both Tchaikovsky and Mahler had shown that it was both possible and persuasive – but Boyle's particular three-movement arrangement is decidedly uncommon. There may be better-known works than Boyle's '*Glencree*' that show a similar organisation – one thinks of E. J. Moeran's Violin Concerto, for example, with its rumbustious central rondo and its serenely contemplative finale – but, interestingly, none of them are symphonies (and Moeran's Concerto did not appear until 1942, fifteen years after Boyle completed '*Glencree*'). Boyle certainly did not set out to be an innovator – there is nothing in her work that suggests she ever thought in such terms. But neither did she allow herself to be intimidated by tradition if creative necessity demanded a more independent approach.[17]

Ex. 10: Symphony No. 1, '*Glencree*', I, bars 1–14

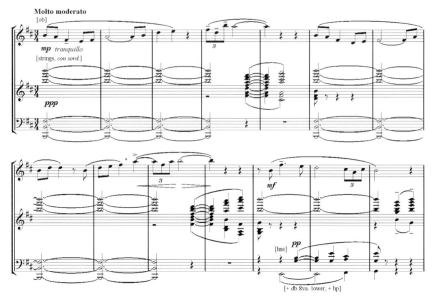

The first movement of the symphony is subtitled 'On Lacken Hill', which probably refers to one of the lower slopes of the Knockree mountain that rises to the south of the Glencree valley. Because of the sustained writing and the leisurely harmonic rhythm, the music unfolds at a slower pace than the composer's tempo direction of *Molto moderato* might initially suggest. As indicated above, the structure of the movement has little to do with conventional sonata form, and the material is lyrical in conception rather than dramatic. The overall design could be described as ternary, allowing for the fact that the two principal thematic blocks of the opening section are reversed in the reprise, which results in an A/B-C-B¹/A¹ structure.

'On Lacken Hill' commences with a long, plaintive oboe solo etched against a background of high, sustained violins underpinned by cellos and double basses (Ex. 10). This material is developed into an initial paragraph of thirty-one bars that confines itself entirely to the diatonic pitches of an Aeolian B minor, the principal tonality of the movement. The first chromatic shift occurs in bar thirty-two when the chord of C major precipitates a sudden change of mood that signals the start of the B section. In a well-calculated contrast to the opening, the tonality is now destabilised and the spacious progressions are endowed with a certain austere grandeur (Ex. 11).

The music becomes increasingly unsettled and is gradually worked up to a substantial climax. But this is short-lived and quickly subsides into the *Più lento, tranquillo* of the central C section, which is articulated by a new idea

Ex. 11: Symphony No. 1, '*Glencree*', I, bars 32–38

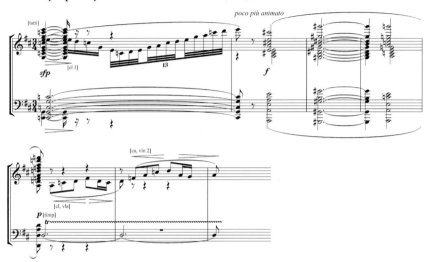

(Ex. 12). The atmosphere of calm with which this new section commences, however, is dispelled as the music again grows restless. It rises to an even more forceful climax that culminates in the return of the second idea, B[1], now so radically abbreviated, however, that it functions as little more than a link to A[1]. With the recapitulation of the opening paragraph, the Aeolian B minor is restored, as is the tranquil atmosphere with which the symphony began. This material is modified and extended to bring the movement to a close – thus obviating the need for a separate coda – and it fades out on a very soft, widely spaced B minor chord in which divided violins and violas float high above the bass, conveying by the simplest means both a marvellous sense of distance and a feeling of profound peace.

Ex. 12: Symphony No. 1, '*Glencree*', I, bars 58–63

In contrast to the bright, *plein air* feel of 'On Lacken Hill', the second movement is a night piece. Entitled 'Nightwinds in the Valley', the mood of this *Allegro molto* is sombre and the atmosphere turbulent and fitful; it represents the dark core of the symphony, a centre of disturbance that acts as a foil to the serenity of the outer movements. In broad terms, the movement is cast as a scherzo and trio – A-B-A[1] – although the structure of the component subsections does not conform to any established plan. Three distinct ideas are announced in the opening eight bars (labelled *a*, *b* and *c* in Ex. 13): the first two comprise fragments of rising, semiquaver chromatic scales followed by a jig-like motif in the bass under sustained harmonies; and after a varied repeat of the scale fragments we hear a new duplet figure, again in the bass. The A section (scherzo) is based almost exclusively on a free working-out of these three ideas, which are repeated and developed against a kaleidoscopic background of shifting chromatic harmonies. The opening of the movement and the key signature of two flats suggest that the basic tonal centre is a modal G minor. In practice, however, the harmony is unstable throughout, reflecting the stormy nature of the music, and the one concession to orthodox tonal organisation is the move to the dominant before the commencement of the trio.

Ex. 13: Symphony No. 1, '*Glencree*', II, bars 1–8

The trio itself is marked *Tranquillo*, and it represents a lull, a moment of respite in the middle of the tempest (Ex. 14). But despite the relative calm, the shift of tonality to the even darker region of E flat minor (modal) continues to lend an ominous, oppressive feel to the music. The trio leads directly into the reprise of scherzo (A¹), in which the opening ideas are re-developed into the principal climax of the movement. But the storm eventually plays itself out and, referring briefly to the main theme of the trio, a short coda brings 'Nightwinds in the Valley' to a quiet end, the final bright G major harmony suggesting the abatement of the wind, the clearing of the skies and, perhaps, the first rays of dawn.

The third movement, 'Above Lough Bray', is a contemplative *Adagio* in which the B minor (modal) tonality is restored. In seeking to create an atmosphere that is similar to the serene mood of the opening of the symphony but yet distinct from it, Boyle imbues the music with a new sense of stillness that succeeds in bringing before the mind's eye, so to speak, fresh aspects of an already familiar landscape. Boyle's particular strength as a composer lies in her ability to reveal the rich, subtle differentiations contained in quiet moods and gentle understatement and, like the County Wicklow countryside that inspired it, this music is entirely without flashiness or superficial brilliance.

Ex. 14: Symphony No. 1, '*Glencree*', II, bars 77–85

'Above Lough Bray' opens *molto tranquillo* with a soft, *tremolando* B minor chord on the strings, over which is suspended a characteristic descending

Ex. 15: Symphony No. 1, '*Glencree*', III, 1–9

Ex. 16: Symphony No. 1, '*Glencree*', III, bars 23–27

melody on the first violins. To this lyrical idea a short, detached figure is
appended in the bass (*a* and *b* in Ex. 15), and together they constitute the
principal material of the first section, A, of the movement. After a varied repeat
of both elements, a new subsidiary motif is heard (Ex. 16), which rounds off the
paragraph and, followed by a final enunciation of *b*, leads directly to the next
section, B. Apart from a few transient chromatic inflections, the first paragraph
is almost entirely diatonic. Unusually, and in contradiction to the customary
expectation of tonal contrast at this point, the B section is similarly diatonic
throughout. The only concession to tonal movement is the re-orientation
of the mode from Aeolian on B to Phrygian on F sharp. But this change is
minimal: although F sharp is now the centre, the diatonic scale from which
both modes are derived remains unchanged. The section is articulated by a
new theme on the cor anglais and characterised by rippling harp figuration
throughout (Ex. 17). To ensure sufficient interest, Boyle is entirely reliant on
the development of salient thematic shapes derived from this idea as well as
on the continually evolving textures, although the dynamic level scarcely rises
above *mezzo piano*. This tonal strategy is maintained as the music moves into
the third paragraph, C (opening shown in Ex. 18). The diatonic scale is still
unchanged, but the music is now centred more on D, in a manner vaguely
suggestive of the relative major of the initial B minor.

Ex. 17: Symphony No. 1, '*Glencree*', III, bars 29–33

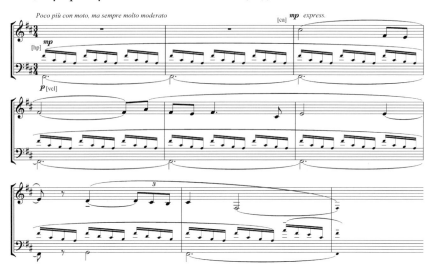

Ex. 18: Symphony No. 1, '*Glencree*', III, bars 76–80

Despite the fact that these three paragraphs – A, B and C – comprise the entire exposition of the movement, tonally speaking virtually nothing has happened. This is an unusual and indeed a risky compositional strategy. In the interest, presumably, of maintaining the greatest possible consistency of feeling and mood, Boyle has jeopardised the very capacity of the music to sustain the listener's interest. Clearly, something must now happen that will break the diatonic spell. Boyle is perfectly aware of this, and in a complete reversal of standard practice, she defers all tonal contrast and modulatory interest until the recapitulation.

All three principal sections – A, B and C – are recapitulated in the order in which they were first heard. The material of the final paragraph of the exposition, C, is developed to lead directly into A[1], which commences just as the tonality shifts abruptly to the Aeolian mode on D. In the context, this is a dramatic move, and although all three of its constituent elements duly make an appearance, their presentation is modified to reflect the darker tonal region:

the mood of the music has become more troubled, suggesting, perhaps, that the skies have become clouded above Lough Bray and the surface of the waters disturbed.

Although still Phrygian, the B¹ section is now recapitulated a fifth lower than before so that B returns as the central pitch while the pervasive C naturals maintain a slightly sombre harmonic colouring. The most surprising move of all is the appearance of C¹ in B major, the 'tonic major' so to speak. In making this move, Boyle echoes standard classical practice where, in minor keys, material first heard in the relative major (as, roughly speaking, the C section originally was) is customarily reprised in the tonic major. As outlined above, the tonal organisation of the present movement owes little or nothing to classical models, and this is a good instance of Boyle's ability to take a commonplace procedure and, by employing it in a radically altered context, to present it in a surprisingly novel light. The movement ends with a short coda, which is based on material from A and over which the shadows continue to hover until, in the final bars, the Aeolian B minor is finally regained.

Ina Boyle had to wait eighteen years before the '*Glencree*' symphony was performed in its entirety in 1945, and then it was heard only in a Radio Éireann broadcast concert. Undaunted, she commenced work on a second major symphonic score in 1929, Symphony No. 2, *The Dream of the Rood*. This was completed the following year and, although she tirelessly sent the manuscript to likely conductors, to her great disappointment not one of them expressed an interest in producing it.

The Dream of the Rood is a substantial three-movement symphony. Despite its literary subtitle, it is a purely instrumental work and the reference to the famous Anglo-Saxon poem – which Boyle reproduces in a modern translation at the beginning of the score – seems to be intended merely to suggest the emotional world of the music. The symphony is not supplied with a programme, nor do the movements have any titles that might indicate which aspects of the poem they may have been meant to illustrate. Nonetheless, the character of each of the three movements does seem to correspond, if only in a general way, to three successive stages of the narrative.

The first movement commences with an introduction, marked *Adagio*, which is perhaps intended to portray the dreaming poet: 'Lo! I will declare the best of dreams which I dreamt in the middle of the night'.[18] The poet tells how he dreamt of the cross on which the Saviour was crucified, and how 'the most excellent tree' began to speak to him. The vigorous, energetic sonata-form *Allegro* that ensues seems intended to suggest the violent events of which the poet is then told. The music is certainly not inconsistent with the description of how the tree is felled, fashioned into the cross and made to bear the Saviour: 'As a rood was I raised up; I bore aloft the mighty King, the Lord of heaven; I durst not stoop'. There is an intensity about this music which suggests that Boyle was creatively engaged in its composition at a deep emotional level; its passionate utterance is expressed in a well-shaped and balanced sonata structure that shows many of the composer's characteristic traits but is also unusually hard-driven and purposeful.

It is likely that the second movement, *Adagio*, corresponds to the passage in the poem that describes the removal of the dead Christ from the cross and the interment of the body in the tomb: 'Then, unhappy in the eventide, they began to sing a dirge'. The marching, five-four *pizzicato* bass of the opening does suggest a funeral procession, and the thematic material has a lamenting quality. The form of the movement is unusual in that it is asymmetrical: the two principal blocks of material, each with two distinct sub-sections, are reprised only in the most perfunctory manner, resulting in an A-B-A¹/B¹ structure, where A¹/B¹ seems more like a coda to the movement rather than a recapitulation of its principal material. But as the passage in question ends with the burial of the rood – 'They buried us in a deep pit' – a full-blown restatement of the main themes may have seemed psychologically redundant.

While it is difficult to say exactly which part of the poem might correspond to the finale's solemn *Grave* introduction, there can be little doubt about the import of the ensuing *Moderato, molto maestoso*, which commences in a buoyant, confident mood with a forthright chorale-like melody harmonised in block chords. The rood, still speaking, admonishes the poet: 'Now I bid thee, my loved man, to declare this vision unto men'. The poet responds: 'Then glad at heart I worshipped the cross with great zeal', and it is with an expression of this gladness that the final movement seems principally to be concerned. The chorale-like theme is succeeded by a second idea that is gentler, more inward in nature and after a slightly faster, somewhat diffuse central section both principal themes are reprised. The beginning of the coda recollects the very opening of the symphony, the poet's dream, and finally a brief reference to the *Grave* introduction brings the work to a quiet conclusion.

Ina Boyle's reputation in Ireland would appear to have been securely launched with the warmly received performance of *Soldiers at Peace* at Woodbrook in February 1920,[19] and the widely reported success of *The Magic Harp* in the Carnegie Trust competition later that year would have confirmed the appearance of a new native composer of promising talent. The fairly lukewarm reviews *Colin Clout* earned when it was played in London in June 1922 may have been disappointing but they kept her name before the public, and in any case they were counterbalanced by the enthusiastic reception given to *The Transfiguration* (1921), a substantial anthem for solo tenor, mixed-voice choir and organ, which was sung at St Patrick's Cathedral in Dublin the following November. Although neither of the two anthems that Boyle published at her own expense in 1915 appear to have been sung during her lifetime, it is surely an indication of the confidence she began to feel in the wake of this positive response to her music that she paid to have *The Transfiguration* published by Novello & Co. but, sadly, the investment does not seem to have resulted in further performances.

The Transfiguration, the text of which was compiled for Boyle by Henry Kingsmill Moore, Canon of St Patrick's Cathedral in Dublin, falls into three principal sections: the first is a setting of verses from the Gospel of St Matthew (17:1–3, 5) in which an opening narration for solo tenor leads to a very effective entry of the choir at the words 'And behold Moses and Elias appeared in glory'; the second is a fairly elaborate setting of 'Glory to God in the highest' for divided sopranos and altos; and the concluding section consists of a setting of verses from Psalm 104 (1–2, 31, 35) in which the choir opens out into double chorus for a splendid antiphonal climax – 'Praise thou the Lord, O my soul!' – before returning to four parts for the triumphant final bars. It is by no means an easy work to sing: the division of the lines would certainly stretch the resources of the average cathedral choir, and it is interesting to note that Boyle acknowledges this by authorising the performance of a shorter version in which the second section may be omitted altogether. Having said this, it is nonetheless expertly written, full of well-calculated dramatic moments and perfectly suited to liturgical performance.

The 1930s were dispiriting years for Ina Boyle. The bright promise of the 1920s seemed to have quickly dimmed and there no longer appeared to be much interest in her work. With one or two short choral pieces, however, she did succeed in keeping her name before the public to some extent. In 1930, a hymn, *Service and Strength* (1929), with words by Christina Rossetti, was published in *Songs of Praise* by Oxford University Press; and in 1935 *A Spanish Pastoral* (1931), a setting of a text by St Teresa of Avila in a translation by Arthur Symons, was accepted by Stainer & Bell. The most interesting of the choral works from this period, however, are the *Gaelic Hymns*, five of which were published (with a subvention by Boyle) by J. & W. Chester in 1930. These were selected from sixteen original settings, fourteen of which had been written between 1923 and 1924 with an additional two composed in 1929.[20] All of them are for unaccompanied voices, although there is considerable variation in the disposition of forces from piece to piece – ranging from mixed-voice chorus in six parts to both male- and female-voice chorus in four parts – and several of them also feature a soloist (alto or bass). The word 'Gaelic' in the title refers to Scots Gaelic, and Boyle chose the texts from *Carmina Gadelica*, a collection of traditional prayers, hymns and blessings collected in the Gaelic-speaking regions of Scotland between 1860 and 1909 by Alexander Carmichael, who translated and published a selection of them in two volumes in 1900.[21]

The five published pieces are: (i) 'Jesu, Thou Son of Mary', (ii) 'The Guardian Angel', (iii) 'The Light'ner of the Stars', (iv) 'The Soul-Leading (A Gaelic Blessing)' and (v) 'Soul Peace (A Death Blessing)'. Some of these hymns received several performances during Boyle's lifetime, and during the early 1930s they may well have been the only works of hers to be heard at all. As the reviews quoted in the first part of this volume suggest,[22] each individual hymn is well written and attractive in itself but if they are performed as a set they can seem somewhat monotonous. Four of the five are in a slow tempo (ranging between *Lento moderato* and *Adagio*), the exception being the third, 'The Light'ner of the Stars', which alone is marked *Allegro*. Moreover, three of them have very similar textures in which a solo alto voice is set against a choral background that is more or less straightforwardly homophonic. There is, however, no reason to believe that Boyle intended the hymns to be sung together in the order in which they were published, as a kind of choral suite, and a selection of, say, three of them – with the 'The Light'ner of the Stars' as the centrepiece to ensure maximum variety of tempo and texture – might make a more viable concert item.

Ex. 19: *Gaelic Hymns*, 1, 'Jesu, Thou Son of Mary', bars 1–11

The first hymn, 'Jesu, Thou Son of Mary', is in six parts (SSATTB) and it opens with effective antiphonal writing between male voices that sing the main text and female voices that respond with 'Amen' (Ex. 19). This approach changes about halfway through; the recurring 'Amen' is still used to bind the music together, but it is now dispersed throughout the texture until eventually it is taken up by all the voices together in a brief coda. 'The Guardian Angel', the second hymn, is simply but imaginatively conceived for alto solo and male voices, and the contrasting tone colours are tellingly exploited. As mentioned above, the only fast piece of the five is the third, 'The Light'ner of the Stars', which is also for six-part chorus. This is the most substantial and elaborately worked setting of the five: the six-part writing is particularly well handled and the balance between a homophonic, chordal style and more flowing contrapuntal material is very finely judged throughout (Ex. 20).

Ex. 20: *Gaelic Hymns*, 3, 'The Light'ner of the Stars', bars 1–9

The alto solo is again featured in the fourth piece, 'The Soul-Leading', and although this time it is offset against four-part mixed voices rather than male voices, it is very similar to the second hymn in its general conception. Unfortunately, Boyle adopts the same approach for the fifth hymn, 'Soul Peace', even if the textures are a little more diversified, with the final section being effectively laid out for five-part choir.

Notwithstanding the discouragement of hearing very little of her work performed, Boyle's tenacity of purpose remained unshakable. In addition to a number of slighter pieces, between 1930 and 1940 she produced some half a dozen substantial orchestral works. The most noteworthy of these are three short ballets, each lasting about thirty minutes: *Virgilian Suite* (1930–31), *The Dance of Death* (1935–36) and *The Vision of Er* (1938–39). In her efforts to have them produced she sent the scores to the Camargo Society, to Marie Rambert (via the pianist Charles Lynch), to Cepta Cullen, who ran the Irish Ballet Club in Dublin, and to Constant Lambert at Sadlers Wells, and while the replies that she received were, on the whole, kind and by no means dismissive, the works never reached the stage and, indeed, apart from two extracts performed in Dublin in 1949 and 1950, none of the music has been heard at all.[23]

Both the title, *Virgilian Suite*, and the subtitle, 'A ballet suite for small orchestra based on the Eclogues of Virgil', suggest a work composed in the style of ballet music rather than a ballet score proper.[24] But Boyle envisaged it as a work for the stage, and the manuscript is prefaced with a brief scenario for each of the four constituent movements together with a list of dancing roles that includes eight soloists and a corps de ballet of 'Nymphs, Fauns & Satyrs & dancers representing Earth, Sea, Cloud & Flame'. That she had a clear picture in her mind of how the music might be realised theatrically is evident from the detailed descriptions of the action that she inserted throughout the score. There is no continuous narrative. The four movements are derived from different eclogues and each represents a separate scene and features its own individual characters. In the first scene (from Virgil's first eclogue) Meliboeus, who is grief-stricken at being driven from home and country, encounters Tityrus, who is permitted to remain; in the second scene (from the fifth eclogue), a group of Nymphs build an altar to honour the slain Daphnis; in the third (from the sixth eclogue), a drunken Silenus sings a song about the formation of the world from the elements of earth, water, air and fire; and in the last scene (derived from a passing allusion in the eighth eclogue) Damon plays a tune on his pipes and is overheard by Pan.

These slight, seemingly inconsequential classical vignettes may not offer much by way of theatrical interest, but many successful ballets have been suspended from frameworks that are hardly less slender. The crucial question is whether the score could be realised in terms of viable choreography, and this is where the doubt arises. Despite the descriptive notes detailing the action as she imagined it, Boyle seems to have approached the task as though she were composing a work for concert performance rather than writing music for the dance, and it is difficult to imagine how the score might be translated into effective theatre. Not only does each movement sustain a single mood throughout, but also the more or less uniform pace of the music would most likely prove unsatisfactory from the choreographic point of view. In addition, three of the four movements are in a slow tempo – with many rhapsodic woodwind solos of the kind associated with shepherds and pastoral scenes generally – and there is little rhythmic vitality. The exception is the third movement, which is cast as an Introduction and Fugue, and although musically it is perhaps the most interesting movement of the four, it is unusual to find a fugue in a ballet score – probably because it also presents serious problems for a choreographer.

The Dance of Death, described by Boyle as 'A Masque', is an altogether more interesting work. In all likelihood, Boyle got the idea from Vaughan Williams' *Job*, subtitled 'A Masque for Dancing', which was first heard in a concert performance in 1930 and staged by the Camargo Society the following year. Just as Vaughan Williams found his inspiration in William Blake's illustrations for *The Book of Job*, so Boyle turned to Hans Holbein the Younger (1497–1543), whose famous series of woodcuts depicting 'The Dance of Death' was first published in 1538.[25] These woodcuts show death in the form of a grimacing skeleton attending upon personages of all types and from all walks of life, ranging from Pope and Emperor to Idiot and Beggar. Boyle chose twenty-two of these designs as the basis for seventeen short scenes (a few scenes involve more than one character), and she supplied the score with brief descriptions of how the woodcuts might be realised in terms of stage action. These seventeen scenes are framed by a Prelude in which skeletons (representing individual deaths) emerge from the tomb playing various musical instruments, and a Finale that shows all the previously depicted personages, each attended by his or her own death, taking part in a stately dance, *Grave, tempo di ciaccona*. As Boyle envisaged it, a production of the work would require substantial resources: it is scored for full orchestra (with cued parts for bagpipe and tenor voice),[26] it requires a large number of dancers (there are twenty-four principal as well as thirteen minor parts), and it assumes fairly elaborate staging.

Musically, the manner in which Boyle handles the subject is highly ingenious, and from the point of view of sheer compositional technique *The Dance of Death* is undoubtedly one of her most accomplished works. Featured somewhere in each of Holbein's woodcuts is the image of an hourglass, a recurring motif that symbolises the passing of time and the inevitability of death. Boyle begins the masque with what she calls 'The Theme of Death', which is heard before the curtain rises. And in a clever, conscious parallel to Holbein's omnipresent hourglass, the ensuing score is structured as a set of variations on this theme. It thus constitutes a permanent feature of the work while at the same time its different embodiments mirror the changing circumstances of death's appearances as depicted in the woodcuts. In other words, Boyle chose a compositional procedure that would allow the reduplication in musical terms of the way in which Holbein's overall design is executed. The theme itself (Ex. 21), with its echoes of the *Dies irae*, is very well suited to its purpose: it is a brief, neutral idea – but with one outstanding, easily identifiable chromatic moment – that is perfectly adaptable to a wide range of musical situations. Boyle's treatment of it is extremely resourceful: modified rhythmically, it frequently appears as a straightforward melodic idea, as in Variation I, Prelude:

'The Cemetery', for example, where it is treated imitatively (Ex. 22); or its constituent pitches can be widely separated as the structuring points in a more freely conceived episode as in Variation II, 'The Pope' (Ex. 23); it appears in inversion in Variation IX, 'The Nun'; is employed as a *cantus firmus* in Variation VI, 'The Bishop'; and in the chaconne, or *ciaccona* of the Finale it is transformed into the recurring ground for what in itself is a majestic, self-contained set of polyphonic variations (Ex. 24). As an example of disciplined, technical skill in the service of creative imagination *The Dance of Death* is unquestionably an impressive achievement.

Ex. 21: *The Dance of Death*, 'Theme of Death (The Hourglass in Holbein)'

Ex. 22: *The Dance of Death*, Variation I, Prelude: 'The Cemetery', bars 1–9

Ex. 23: *The Dance of Death*, Variation II, 'The Pope', bars 1–10

Ex. 24: *The Dance of Death*, Finale: 'The Dance of Death', bars 1–8

[from the composer's piano score]

Whether the masque would prove theatrically effective, however, is difficult to say. Unlike the *Virgilian Suite*, it certainly offers a potential choreographer more varied material to work with. Boyle has evidently given careful consideration to the contrast between the different variations in terms of tonality, tempo and texture. The pacing of the work is also well thought out: there is a good balance of relative duration and intensity in the way the variations are ordered, and while the earlier ones are more often separated by pauses or rests (although a few of them are linked), as the work moves towards a conclusion they are run together continuously so that the Finale emerges as the effective culmination of the work as a whole. While theatrically this might not be enough to outweigh the difficulty of making a coherent entertainment out of a lengthy series of brief individual scenes, there is no reason to doubt its effectiveness from the purely musical point of view. As an orchestral work in the form of a theme and variations, it would certainly make a viable concert piece.

Ina Boyle described her third ballet as 'A Mimed Drama with Music founded on Plato's *Republic*, Book X'. That the austere abstractions of a great philosopher could have any point of contact with the world of ballet seems at first a somewhat surprising idea, but Plato's *Republic* ends – as do some of his other dialogues – with a myth. In this case it is 'The Vision of Er', the tale of a warrior who has been slain on the battlefield, but returns to life on the twelfth day to recount what he has seen in the other world. The myth represents what the philosopher believes to be a truth, but a truth that cannot be established by philosophical inquiry or by argument. Myth begins, in other words, at the point where philosophy proper ceases: in order to convey what is intuited but cannot be demonstrated, the imagination reaches out beyond reason to create a symbolic embodiment of belief. Emotionally rarefied and elevated in tone though the resultant work may be, Plato's narrative is certainly amenable to musical and theatrical treatment and what, on the face of it, might seem a misguided attempt on the part of the composer to devise an entertainment based on a dry philosophical treatise is, in fact, an entirely practical proposition. Of course, Boyle was not the first composer to attempt this: Richard Strauss and Frederick Delius, for example, both sought inspiration in the writings of Friedrich Nietzsche. But, like 'The Vision of Er', Nietzsche's *Also sprach Zarathustra* is a philosophical myth rather than a rigorous philosophical investigation, and from the composer's point of view is rewarding for exactly the same reasons.

'The Vision of Er' recounts Plato's version of the ancient doctrine of the transmigration of souls: according to their conduct while on earth, the souls of the dead are assigned either to reward or punishment for an allotted period until the time comes for them to be re-born into a new life. (The souls of animals have the same power of choice and may be born again as men, just as men may be reincarnated as animals if they so desire.) Plato's story mentions enough individual characters whose situations are recounted with just sufficient colour and incident to make a viable dramatic representation feasible. Boyle's adaptation is skilful and her selection and arrangement of the material shows a keen instinct for what will best suit her purpose. Her envisioning of the work is comprehensive, and not only is the full score prefaced with six carefully executed watercolours depicting various moments in the drama, there is also a portfolio containing several supplementary paintings amongst her papers in Trinity College Dublin. The ballet is scored for standard full orchestra with the addition of three solo female voices (for which instrumental cues are, however, provided); the cast comprises fifteen solo roles (some of which are comparatively minor), as well as a *corps de ballet* of Souls and Angels; and the staging requires three changes of scene.

The work opens with a short Prelude (*Grave*), which is directed to be played before a dark inner curtain. It is the twelfth day after the death of Er and his body, which has not suffered corruption, lies on its funeral pyre. To the wonder of the assembled mourners, Er returns to life, and as he commences his account of what he has witnessed while dead the inner curtain rises on Scene I. The setting is a mysterious place with four openings or entrances, two leading down into the earth and two leading up to the heavens above. Three judges sit in the centre and the souls of the newly dead are brought before them to receive their sentences: the just are directed to ascend by the upward path to heaven, and the unjust to descend by the lower into the earth. From the second pair of openings – one also from above and one from below – other souls then emerge, 'some ascending out of the earth dusty and worn with travel, some descending out of heaven clean and bright'.[27] These are the souls of those who have completed their sojourn in the other world, and are now ready to be re-born into life.

This comprises the initial section of Scene I, and Boyle has provided music that conveys the calm orderliness of supernaturally regulated events with uncanny insight. Based on an unhurried, largely conjunct melody in the bass and a serene complementary idea on the upper strings (in a modal A minor, the principal tonality of the work), she builds up a superbly sustained paragraph (*Lento ma non troppo*) that depicts the eternal coming and going of the souls. Er describes how the judges informed him that 'he was to be the messenger that would carry the report of the other world to men',[28] and he tells how he overheard two spirits discussing the fate of Ardiaeus the Tyrant, whose crimes were so great that his torments would never end. Boyle realised that this internally recounted history would provide her with a good opportunity to introduce a sharply contrasted episode, and accordingly she transposed it to the foreground action of her ballet. The tempo increases to *Più mosso (allegro)*, and Ardiaeus and his companions, who are uncouth and insolent in manner, enter noisily. The music – boisterous, detached quaver passagework in the strings set against thematic material with wide, angular leaps – reflects their rough behaviour. These ideas are built up into an impressive climax as Ardiaeus and his companions try to force their way into the place of judgement. But the mouth of the cavern through which they must ascend, instead of admitting them, gives a terrifying roar, whereupon they are seized and dragged away 'to be cast into Tartarus'.[29]

After the tumult, calm returns (*Andante sostenuto, molto tranquillo*) and the souls begin to assemble in a peaceful meadow: they rest; acquaintances recognise one another, embrace and converse; and all exchange accounts of their experiences, whether of punishment below or of heavenly bliss above. This third episode leads naturally to the final moments of the scene when, to a reprise of the opening ideas, the souls form themselves into a company and begin to move forward to the next stage of their journey.

In Scene II, the stage is split into two levels: on the lower level we see a cave beneath the earth where Necessity sits enthroned, and on the upper we see the three fates – Lachesis, Clotho and Atropos – who sing of the past, present, and future. Running vertically through both levels is a pillar of light. In the midst of this light the ends of chains that are let down from heaven are visible, from which the spindle of Necessity is suspended. The scene opens with a wordless vocalise by the three solo female voices depicting the singing of the fates (*Allegro moderato*), and the murmuring semiquaver accompaniment suggests their ceaseless spinning. The opening ideas of Scene I are recalled as the company of souls enters, accompanied now by a Prophet (*Lento solonelle* [*sic*]) who delivers himself of a vigorous exhortation (*Adagio*). He casts lots before them and each soul takes up the lot that falls nearest to him. The Prophet then receives the patterns of future lives from Lachesis and spreads them out so that the souls can come forward, according to the order in which the lots fell, and make their choices.

The central episode of the scene, The Choosing of Souls, now ensues. Several well-known mythological personages appear in Er's narrative as representative both of the kinds of choices that are made and of the reasons that motivate them. Boyle focuses on these individuals and with considerable inventiveness devises an episode constructed as a theme and variations, where each variation depicts a single character in the act of selecting his future life. The Theme (*Allegro, ma non troppo*) is thus succeeded by Variation I, which depicts Orpheus electing to be re-born as a swan; Variation II, Ajax as a lion (*Allegro*); Variation III, Atalanta as an athlete (*Con moto, poco capriccio*); and Variation IV, Thersites the Jester as a monkey (*Allegretto*). In the final variation, V, which is a fugue (*Allegro moderato*), the remainder of the souls come forward, until at the climax we see the wise Odysseus choose to be re-born as 'a private man who had no cares'.[30] In the concluding episode of the scene, The Satisfaction of the Fates, each soul, having made its choice, is assigned an Angel. To a recapitulation of the opening vocalise and the accompanying motif of spinning, the souls then come before Clotho, who passes them under the spindle; thence to Atropos who makes the threads unalterable; and finally they are all led under the throne of Necessity where they wait.

Scene III (*Molto adagio*), which is set on the banks of the river Lethe, is considerably shorter than the first two scenes and seems to function more like an epilogue to the work as a whole. Having endured a march through scorching heat on the plain of forgetfulness, the souls enter wearily, again to music that reprises material from Scene I. They are instructed to drink of the river water, whereupon they forget all things. They sleep. But their repose is abruptly shattered by a thunderstorm and an earthquake, and the Angels come forward to lead them to the background, where each is seen for a brief moment outlined against the light before leaping to his new birth alone. The Angels remain behind, and the music dies away with a final reminiscence of the opening ideas and a concluding evocation of the serene eternal order against which all the events have taken place.

The Vision of Er must rank as one of Ina Boyle's most fully realised and polished creations: the music is memorable, tightly constructed and tellingly orchestrated. It is undoubtedly the finest of the three dance scores. Whether or not a choreographer might have reservations about the symphonic character of the music is a separate issue. Symphonically conceived dance scores have been successfully choreographed and staged in the past, however (one thinks of Ravel's *Daphnis et Chloé*, for example), and while it is true that there is a good deal of slow music in *The Vision of Er*, on the whole, contrasts in tempo and pacing are well managed throughout. Both because of its thematic vividness and its compelling overall structural coherence, it would make an effective concert piece, even more so than *The Dance of Death*, especially if, instead of the stage representation, a suitable accompanying spoken narration was devised to ensure that the music lost none of its dramatic immediacy.

Apart from the *Elegy* for violoncello and orchestra (or piano) of 1913, Ina Boyle composed three other concertante works. The first of them, *Phantasy* for violin and chamber orchestra, was written in 1926, and the second, *Psalm* for violoncello and orchestra, was written in 1927 and entered for what was to be the final Carnegie Trust competition the following year (it was not successful). The third work, and by far the most important, is the Concerto for Violin and Orchestra, which was completed in 1933 and revised to some extent in 1935.

Although in its self-effacing avoidance of all technical brilliance it is unlikely to recommend itself to many soloists, the Violin Concerto is a gentle, attractive work with a curiously unworldly atmosphere. It also seems to have had a particular personal significance for the composer. On a prefatory page of the manuscript Boyle pasted a newspaper clipping of a poem by Pamela Grey of Fallodon: "'All Souls Flower': A Christmas Carol'.[31] Boyle, it seems, occasionally composed songs as birthday or Christmas gifts for her mother, and her setting of this carol for voice and piano in 1928 was the last of these offerings to be written before her mother's death four years later. Clearly, the song retained strong associations for her as she used material from it in the third movement of the Concerto, which is dedicated to her mother's memory.

Apart from these private associations, Boyle's decision to attach the clipping to the score may also have been intended to convey her expressive intentions in composing it. Referring to the image of the 'Flower', lines from the poem like: 'So sweet a sap runs in its veins / As may subdue all griefs or pains'; or: 'It grows beside a bitter Tree, / O Flower of Grace! / That is, for all our sins, solace', certainly reflect the sweet, unclouded serenity of the music. And the concerto is unusual in that it is singularly free of the kind of conflicts and oppositions – thematic, harmonic and tonal – that one might expect to find in such an extended concertante work. But if one approaches the piece as a meditation on the theme of Pamela Grey's carol – a meditation on the mystery of Christmas – rather than as a drama, then the absence of conflict no longer seems quite so puzzling.

A further aspect of this association with Christmas – echoed, perhaps, in the dedication to the composer's mother – are the sorrows as well as the joys of the motherhood of Mary, which are suggested by references to the 'bitter Tree' for example, as already quoted, or 'O lovely Flower! / Blossom and Thorn of Mary's bower'. And one wonders if it can be purely by accident that the opening harmonies of the concerto are virtually the same as the distinctive progression heard at the beginning of Palestrina's setting of the *Stabat Mater*, the thirteenth-century hymn depicting the sorrowing Virgin at the foot of the cross: an A major chord followed by the chords of G major and F major.

Whether this evocation of the *Stabat Mater* is fortuitous or by design, it is interesting to note the similar atmosphere of rapt, almost disembodied contemplation that permeates much of the concerto. The creation of this untroubled mood is made possible, of course, by Boyle's diatonic, essentially triadic harmonic language as well as by her handling of tonality, which often recalls the fluid modal organisation of sixteenth-century polyphony – although extended, obviously, to encompass more remote tonal regions and accommodate a greater degree of dissonance. In several respects, the work seems to owe more to the structural techniques of the sixteenth-century motet than to the conventions of the modern instrumental concerto. Much of this no doubt reflects the influence of Vaughan Williams on Boyle's general compositional approach, although Vaughan Williams never essayed a concerto in which virtuosic display is renounced as completely as it is here. But while this influence is important it is not overwhelming, and the work possesses an unaffected sincerity of utterance and a simple directness of style that is entirely Boyle's own.

The first movement, *Lento, ma non troppo*, is straightforward in its organisation, and although the A-B-A^1-B^1 structure might at first suggest a sonata form without development, the oppositional dynamic of sonata procedures is, as already noted, entirely absent. The movement opens with the sequence of harmonies described above delivered *piano* by the orchestra (the central G major chord of the Palestrina progression amplified here by an additional, closely related chord of E minor), as shown in Ex. 25. The four-note motif outlined on the first violins (*x* in Ex. 25) – C-sharp-B-G-A – supplies a basic shape from which rhythmic and intervallic variants are derived to create much of the thematic material of both the A and A^1 sections. This motif (together with its accompanying harmonies) is immediately restated in a rhythmically condensed form, and when the soloist enters three bars later it is with yet a third variant, which blossoms into a brief cadenza-like passage. The ensuing paragraph (also shown in Ex. 25) is a varied repeat of the first, and affords a very clear example of Boyle's technique of motivic manipulation, by which details are altered while the basic identity of the ideas is retained. This process of unemphatic but continuous thematic mutation is Boyle's preferred method of development and is in evidence throughout.

The second group of ideas, B (Ex. 26), is designed less as a contrast to the opening than as an intensification of the prevailing mood of the movement.

Ex. 25: Violin Concerto, I, bars 1–20

The modified restatement of the violin's oscillating figure leads the music to fresh tonal regions for the first time and, supplemented by a rising four-note idea which is developed at some length, it issues in a climax based on motif x, now a tone lower than at the opening of the concerto. Further treatment of the rising four-note figure then leads directly to the recapitulation, A^1.

Apart from some rescoring, some slight internal reorganisation and the reshaping of the soloist's brief cadenza passages, A^1 is, in substance, very

Ex. 26: Violin Concerto, I, bars 29–38

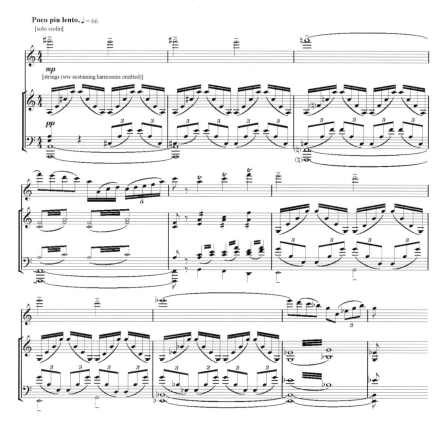

similar to A. While the proportions of B¹, however, are virtually the same as B, the tonal organisation is modified to redirect the music back to the basic harmonies of the opening – A major, G major (supplemented by E minor) and F major – especially A major, now quietly established as the tonic, on which the movement comes to a peaceful close.

The concluding chord of the first movement is sustained as a link into the beginning of the second, a poignant, rhapsodic *Adagio*, the opening of which is shown in Ex. 27. The poignancy of the music is partly due to the flatwards shift of tonality – the new centre is a modal G minor – but also to the fact that, despite the changed tonal circumstances, the violin seems unable to relinquish the note A. It returns to this pitch again and again as if to a happy memory, even briefly inspiring the orchestra to recall the A major harmony of the first movement. The form of the movement is elusive, and Boyle avoids clear-cut sectionality in favour of a continuously evolving structure in which a handful of melodic shapes are brought together in ever-new combinations. Nonetheless,

Ex. 27: Violin Concerto, II, bars 1–6

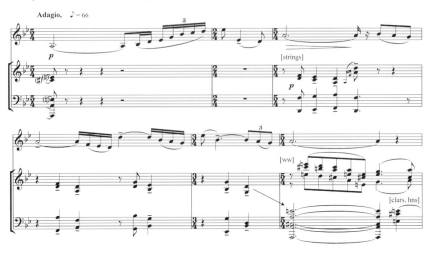

there are a number of more or less identifiable constituent paragraphs. The first
of these sections (commencing as shown in Ex. 27) is unified less by the thematic
content than by the accompaniment, in which units of one or more crotchet
beats are preceded by a quaver anacrusis. Tonally, it is diatonic throughout
with the exception of two moments where the harmony is brightened, as in the
move to the A major chord alluded to above. Although the thematic material
assumes more clearly defined outlines, the same observations are largely true
for the second section. The principal contrast is reserved for the third section,
where the tonality is darkened with the introduction of the pitch A-flat and
where the texture becomes more agitated. The thematic content, although
still derived from existing melodic shapes, now crystallises into clear-cut four-
bar phrases and the solo violin achieves a brief, passionate moment of lyrical
eloquence. The final paragraph both recapitulates certain characteristic features
of the first two sections, albeit greatly condensed and altered, and re-establishes
the prevailing modal G minor. There is no discrete ending to the movement,
however, and a brief transitional passage, *animando e crescendo*, leads directly
to the finale.

Marked *Allegro, ma non troppo*, the finale is cast in simple rondo form in
which the rondo theme alternates with two episodes derived from Boyle's 1928
setting of 'All Souls Flower': A-B-A^1-B^1-A^2-coda. The importance of the poem
for the composer and its significance in assessing the import of the concerto
seems to be confirmed by the fact that Boyle has written the relevant words
into the manuscript over each quotation from the song as it occurs.

Ex. 28: Violin Concerto, III, bars 1–7

The C major in which the movement begins seems somewhat surprising as it emerges from the previous *Adagio*, but it undoubtedly imparts a brisk freshness to the cheerful three-four rondo theme (Ex. 28). This is first announced by the soloist, and the mood of innocent gaiety is maintained by the orchestra as it takes up and develops the material.

The tonality shifts to the brighter region of A major for the first episode, in which the melody of 'All Souls Flower' (covering the first stanza of Pamela Grey's poem) is given to the woodwind with the lightest string accompaniment (Ex. 29). This is decorated with *leggieramente* semiquaver figuration on the solo violin that by the simplest means succeeds in creating an atmosphere of untroubled felicity and radiant spiritual happiness.

An abbreviated return of the rondo theme leads to the second episode, which is now in A-flat and correspondingly more sombre. The melody – a free variant rather than a mere repeat of that heard in the first episode – is now delivered by the soloist with a wistful counterpoint on clarinet and a delicate orchestral background that becomes richer and fuller as the music moves towards the final restatement of the main theme. This commences in A-flat, but as it returns to C the melody associated with lines five and six of the third stanza of 'All Souls Flower' (neither the tune nor the words for the first four lines are featured) is heard on trumpet and trombone in counterpoint against it. For its final entry, the soloist takes up the melody to which the last two lines of the poem are set – 'O Flower of Grace / That is, for all our sins, solace' – and on the word 'Grace' it is expanded into a soaring cadenza. This has the

Ex. 29: Violin Concerto, III, bars 28–32

feeling of being an envoi to the work as a whole, and the orchestra, which accompanies the soloist's concluding phrase, duly picks up the tempo for a final joyous flourish which, as it dies away, brings the concerto to an end on a soft and serene sustained A major chord.

Boyle's disappointment must have been acute when in 1935 the BBC rehearsed the Violin Concerto but ultimately decided not to broadcast it. If the early 1930s was for her a deeply discouraging period, this undoubtedly marked a low moment. As the decade drew to a close, however, there were more positive developments as several significant performances of other works took place. The String Quartet in E minor – which is discussed below – was broadcast by the BBC in 1937, and *Colin Clout* was performed in a landmark concert of music by Irish composers held in Dublin in 1938. This concert, which was given under the auspices of Radio Éireann and conducted by Aloys Fleischmann (who had already programmed *Colin Clout* in a Cork Symphony Orchestra concert two years before), also featured compositions by Fleischmann himself, Frederick May, Elizabeth Maconchy, Hamilton Harty and, as an honorary Irishman, E. J. Moeran. The event was designed to showcase the work of modern Irish composers and, despite Boyle's comparatively low public profile (it was nearly ten years since *The Magic Harp* had received its Irish premiere in 1929, the last time any of her music had been heard in Dublin), her inclusion in the programme was an acknowledgement of her accepted position in contemporary Irish music.[32] This modest, but heartening, trend continued during the 1940s. Not only were there further performances of earlier works like *The Magic Harp* and *Gaelic Hymns* but also, as already mentioned, the complete '*Glencree*' symphony was broadcast on Radio Éireann in 1945, and a vivid and engaging Overture for orchestra, dating from 1933–34, was finally premiered in Dublin in 1948.

In 1942 she composed a short piece for small orchestra, *Wildgeese*, which became one of her most frequently performed compositions during the 1940s, and, although it is a slight work and not by any means one of her best, it is still occasionally heard today. Appropriately described as a 'sketch' by the composer, *Wildgeese* is reminiscent of an old-fashioned watercolour in its gentle understatement and it recalls similar short evocations of nature, such as the well-known *Scene with Cranes* (1903) from Sibelius's incidental music to Arvid Järnefelt's *Kuolema*. The composer prefaced the score with a motto from the Greek poet Alcaeus of Mytilene (in a translation by J. M. Edmonds),[33] which suggests the mood she is attempting to capture: 'What birds are these that come from the ends of the earth and the ocean, wildgeese of motley neck and widespread wing?'

Ex. 30: *Wildgeese*, bars 1–10

Wildgeese opens softly, *Lento misterioso*, with a prefix of two bars in which an important accompaniment figure, which is extensively employed throughout the piece, is heard on the lower strings. D minor, the tonal centre of the work, is clearly asserted at the outset, and with the commencement of the principal thematic material in bar 3 not only is this confirmed as modal (Dorian), but the piquant combination of a D minor triad with an added B is also established as a characteristic sonority of the piece (Ex. 30). The composer relies entirely on freely handled but unobtrusive diatonic dissonance of this kind to alleviate the prevailing D minor harmony until bar 18 when, articulated by a subsidiary contrasting figure, the first decisive harmonic shift occurs. D minor (with the added sixth) now yields twice to its subdominant transposition, but the tonic is immediately reasserted and the first part of the work concludes with a short cumulative passage based on the rhythmic figure first heard in bar 4. There is a return to the Dorian subdominant (on G) for the ensuing *Più lento*, a brief contrasting section characterised by a wistful theme on solo cello (Ex. 31). But it is only after the resumption of the initial tempo in bar 41 that any far-reaching harmonic movement occurs. The comparative tonal stasis of what has gone before creates a context in which the new shifting chromatic progressions acquire considerable expressive force and, harnessed to a purposeful development of the opening idea, they lead quickly to the principal climax of the work. As the tension subsides there is a brief reference to the solo cello melody, now centred on D Dorian, and the short concluding paragraph that follows (*Più lento, molto tranquillo*) functions as a coda to the whole. Here, although the pure D minor harmony of the opening is regained, the enigmatic B is added for the final chord, which suggests that the piece may end with a question mark – recalling for us, perhaps, the quotation from Alcaeus at the beginning of the score.

Ex. 31: *Wildgeese*, bars 29–36

Although Ina Boyle composed a substantial amount of chamber music – there are a dozen works altogether – only two are instrumental while the remainder are vocal works accompanied by chamber ensemble. The first of the instrumental pieces, the *Phantasy* for viola and piano of 1918, was not performed during Boyle's lifetime. The second is the String Quartet in E minor of 1934 (rev. 1937), which, as mentioned above, was broadcast by the BBC in 1937.

The String Quartet affords an excellent example of Boyle's fully developed, diatonic modal style, a compositional idiom largely inseparable from her predilection for gentle, pastoral moods. While her expressive range can encompass both melancholy and merriment, she generally prefers to avoid extremes of emotion. The sinewy muscularity and grittiness with which composers like Vaughan Williams or E. J. Moeran, for example, offset the quiet, meditatively pastoral aspects of their work have no place in her music, and their often harshly dissonant harmonic vocabulary is notably absent. But if the String Quartet exemplifies Boyle's natural expressive restraint, it also demonstrates the success with which she can operate within the limits of this style to create necessary contrasts of atmosphere and feeling across a multi-movement work.

As in the case of the similarly titled *Mass in G minor* by Vaughan Williams, the E minor key designation has no traditional connotations: common-practice dominant harmony is absent as, consequently, are all standard cadential formulae. The central tonality of the quartet is the Aeolian mode on E, which is handled in an essentially diatonic fashion throughout: tonal variety is, for the

Ex. 32: String Quartet in E minor, I, bars 1–17

most part, achieved by simple transpositions of the mode, and the harmonic language, which encompasses a degree of subtle but unobtrusive dissonance, is more frequently derived from the contrapuntal movement of the parts than from any functional chordal relationships.

The first movement, a flowing *Allegro moderato*, is cast in a fairly straightforward sonata form. It opens with a first subject group that comprises three distinct elements (labelled *a*, *b* and *c* in Ex. 32). This initial paragraph is worth considering in some detail as it demonstrates the technical adroitness of which Boyle is capable, something that her comparatively unassertive manner can all too easily cause to be overlooked. In the first place, the harmonic language demonstrates her sure judgement in managing the ebb and flow of freely handled diatonic dissonance. The tonic ninth chord in the first bar, for example, yields gracefully to the seventh chord on C in the second, the momentary resolution of which onto A minor harmony leads inevitably to the B minor of the third. This, of course, is merely a standard I-IV-V progression adapted to the modal idiom, but what might have remained little more than a formula has here been successfully revitalised so that it bears the distinctive stamp of the composer's personality. If, technically, Boyle's music remains innocent of the more *recherché* experimentation of early twentieth century music, her ability to re-imagine the ordinary in fresh and engaging ways is, on the other hand, evident throughout her work.

In her handling of phrase structure, too, Boyle demonstrates a similar kind of deft workmanship. The opening seven-bar phrase, notable for the effortless elegance of its rapid ascent through two and a half octaves, is continued by a related three-bar descending phrase, which is itself provided with a two-bar extension. The balanced irregularity of this construction is very neatly achieved, as is that of the ensuing four-bar idea, *b*, where the salient motif of the first two bars is contracted into the hemiola of the subsequent two. The third idea, *c*, which is characterised by repeated semiquavers, seems at first to serve merely as an appendix to the preceding paragraph, but it acquires an increasingly significant role as the movement unfolds. It also serves to introduce the first accidental – C-sharp – into what is otherwise a completely diatonic passage and thus to herald the coming shift to the dominant.

After an abbreviated counterstatement of *a*, both *b* and *c* are reworked to lead directly to the second subject group (there is no distinct transitional material). This group, in the Aeolian mode on B (the dominant), comprises a lively principal theme in dotted rhythm (shown in Ex. 33 below), which is immediately succeeded by several subsidiary ideas that lead without a break to the central development section. Exploring remoter and darker tonal

Ex. 33: String Quartet in E minor, I, bars 47–52

regions, this mostly concerns itself with the constituent elements of the first subject group. The recapitulation commences with a more intense version of *a*, followed by *b* and *c*, and is duly modified to remain in the tonic region (E minor) for the second group, all the elements of which are also restated. The movement concludes with a meditative coda, again based on ideas from the first group. After a final, somewhat enigmatic allusion to the darker tonalities of the development section, the viola enunciates a single recitative-like phrase that restores the Aeolian mode on E (over a *tremolando* E pedal on the cello), and, coming to rest on the note B, brings the movement to a close in a somewhat questioning manner.

Ex. 34: String Quartet in E minor, II, bars 1–10

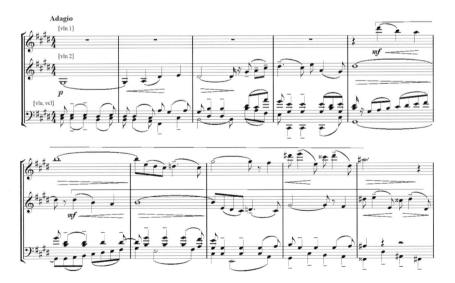

Boyle retains the Aeolian mode as the tonal basis of the second movement, but it is now centred on C-sharp. Cast in three-part form – A-B-A¹ – this plaintive *Adagio* is the emotional core of the quartet. The opening A section, the first ten bars of which are shown in Ex. 34, is characterised by canonic writing: canon at the octave between the two violins gives way after six bars to freer canonic imitation at the fifth between first violin and viola only to disperse subsequently into less systematic thematic echoing. Although tonally fluctuating, the flowing, *molto tranquillo* B section tends to adhere to the Aeolian mode on B as a central reference. Thematically, it consists of the free development of a number of ideas that are loosely derived from the material of A, which is also evoked in the free imitative writing of the central climax. As is Boyle's habit, the material of the opening is drastically curtailed in the A¹ section, which confines itself to a few brief reminiscences before concluding on a hushed C-sharp major chord.

The finale, a vivacious six-eight *Allegro molto*, returns to the Aeolian mode on E and, like the first movement, is also cast in sonata form. It opens less with a recognisable theme than with an assemblage of fragments – a brief rising passage based on a repeated-note figure together with a variant (retrograde) of this repeated-note figure heard against a descending duplet idea (as shown in Ex. 35) – which coalesce into a unified paragraph that comprises the first subject.

Ex. 35: String Quartet in E minor, bars 1–8

Again, as in the first movement, this material is manipulated to lead directly to the second subject, which, while centred on the dominant as before, is now in the Phrygian rather than in the Aeolian mode. The problem with this strategy (as in the finale of the *'Glencree'* symphony discussed above), however, is that it minimises tonal contrast: a new centre (B) may be established, but the spectrum of available diatonic pitches, of course, remains the same. As if in compensation, the second group contains a greater diversity of material than the first. In contrast to the first subject, the principal idea (Ex. 36) is a clear-cut melody and it is supplemented with a number of secondary ideas which introduce discrete chromatic shading to offset the otherwise unrelieved diatonicism.

Ex. 36: String Quartet in E minor, III, bars 23–28

The development section is largely based on the component motifs of the first group and culminates in a sustained, mysterious-sounding passage marked *pianissimo*, which dies away into the beginning of the recapitulation. This, however, is startlingly unusual in its tonal organisation: the restatement of the first group is orthodox, but the decision to recapitulate the second group in the remote region of (Phrygian) G-sharp minor is decidedly problematic. In other words, at the point where, in the traditional understanding of sonata form, tonally dissonant material customarily demands resolution into the tonic key, Boyle chooses instead to introduce the most radical divergence from the central tonality. The entire second group is recapitulated at this remote pitch, and the sole gesture towards ultimate tonal resolution occurs at the beginning of the coda, where the opening idea of the second group is restored to the tonic region before a final flourish brings the work to an end, *fortissimo*, on an E minor chord.

The problem Boyle has created here is not an abstract one, and ignoring tradition as such is not the issue; it is rather that abandoning the principle of tonal equilibrium in a work that is otherwise so unambiguously and transparently tonal compromises the persuasiveness of the musical argument. What Boyle most likely intended was to balance the principal tonality of an Aeolian E minor with a final move to the 'tonic major', more or less as she had done in the finale of the '*Glencree*' symphony. The situation in the symphony, however, is different: a passage initially heard in D major (the relative major, so to speak, of the Aeolian B minor home key) is reprised in B major. In the present case, the tonal centre of the original passage is not G, the relative major, but a Phrygian B, which, when transposed to four sharps, becomes Phrygian G-sharp, and consequently any potential sense of a bright 'tonic major' resolution is skewed. Such a move may not in itself be inconceivable or unmanageable, but in the present context it seems to be a misjudgement. There is simply not sufficient subsequent music to absorb the tonal shock and allow the work to be brought to a fully achieved, satisfactory conclusion. As it stands, the ending seems both premature and somewhat perfunctory. This is a pity, as it undoubtedly mars – although not fatally – one of the composer's most attractive pieces.

Given that Ina Boyle's creative imagination drew so heavily from literature, it is not surprising that a large proportion of her output should consist of vocal music. These works fall into three categories: songs with piano accompaniment, works for solo voice and chamber ensemble, and works for solo voice and orchestra. In the songs with piano accompaniment – of which she composed about sixty or so – Boyle was to some extent hampered by her limitations as a pianist. (Interestingly, she composed no piano music.) Her writing for the instrument is occasionally ineffective – as in her setting of Robert Herrick's *Eternity* (1924) – but even at its best it is rarely more than serviceable in a conventional way. The inescapable consequence of using fairly basic accompaniment textures is that all the interest is focused on the vocal line. And although Boyle is skilful at devising arioso-like contours that are well suited to the clear delivery of the words, she is limited as an inventor of the kind of melody required to lift these pieces out of the ordinary. Her customary neat craftsmanship, nice sense of proportion and instinct for the telling gesture may not ultimately be enough to compensate for a lack of memorability, but some of the songs are nonetheless sufficiently distinguished to reward both singer and audience, like the two Walter de la Mare settings of 1922 (both published by Stainer & Bell), or the later, 1956 settings of the same poet, for example.

The finest of Ina Boyle's vocal works are to be found amongst those with accompaniments for chamber ensemble, in which freedom from the restrictions of the keyboard allowed her imagination far greater scope. Unlike the straightforward lyric settings for voice and piano, however, these tend to be longer pieces, more like extended *scenas* in which the expressive range of the music reflects the greater emotional complexity of the chosen texts. Six of them are scored for solo voice and string quartet, and two of these are particularly noteworthy: *Thinke then, my soule* (1938), with words by John Donne, and *Still falls the rain* (1948), with words by Edith Sitwell.

Although composed about six years or so earlier, Ina Boyle's *Still falls the rain* is probably destined to remain completely overshadowed by Benjamin Britten's more famous setting.[34] This is regrettable, as it is a sensitive and effective treatment of a poem that the composer clearly found deeply moving. It would be foolish to claim that it could stand comparison with Britten's work, which has not only become the definitive setting of the text – even winning the approving poet's rarely bestowed imprimatur – but is also music of supreme technical skill and ingenuity. It is only when the comparison is left aside, however, that Boyle's very different work can be appreciated for what it is. Her reading of Sitwell's poem is intensely personal, and the music that embodies her response to it not only carries conviction, but also has genuine sweep and authority. Fortunately, no such considerations impinge on *Thinke then, my soule*,[35] a work that in some respects ranks amongst her finest achievements. She herself understood this, and paid to have the score published by Oxford University Press in 1939. This time, happily, the investment was justified and the piece received several performances.

In *Thinke then, my soule* a deep emotional engagement on the part of the composer is matched by a high level of inspiration. There is also a particularly felicitous conjunction between the text and her chosen medium. The sustained, linear style of the accompaniment, for example, which would not make for particularly good piano writing, is well suited to stringed instruments, and the resultant sonorities have an intimacy appropriate to the personal, confessional nature of the poem. Although the textures are for the most part simple, they are nonetheless skilfully varied and developed throughout the piece to suggest the poet's increasingly feverish imaginings as he confronts the inevitability of death. Cast in an F-sharp minor that seems to hover anxiously between its modal and tonal forms (the leading note, E-sharp, makes fleeting, but indeterminate appearances), the work commences with a substantial introductory paragraph for the strings (thirty-two bars of tempo *Grave*), which immediately establishes the prevailing mood of fretfulness and disquiet. The remainder of the piece is then structured in three linked sections that correspond to Boyle's division of the lines she selected from Donne's *The Second Anniversarie*. In each of these sections the tenor commences on a different note of the ascending F-sharp minor triad in turn – F-sharp, A and C-sharp – which effectively conveys by the simplest means the poet's mounting horror as the thought of death presses upon him.

Although initially the tone of the first section is calm – 'Thinke then, My soule, that death is but a Groome' – an unmistakable sense of disturbance begins to pervade the concluding bars. In the second section – 'Thinke thy selfe labouring now with broken breath' – not only is a greater sense of urgency created by the tenor beginning a third higher on the note A, but the heightened tension is also reflected in the restless textures as well as in the shift of the tonal centre to F (the enharmonic equivalent of the elusive leading note). For the concluding section, *Più largamente*, the tonic F-sharp is regained, and against a strident pealing motif on the upper strings the soloist delivers the ominous words 'Thinke that thou hears't thy knell' on the note C-sharp (dramatically dropping an octave on the word 'knell'), from which point the music quickly rises to a searing climax.

Boyle demonstrates acute psychological perception in the way she brings the work to a conclusion. At the point of greatest strain all the frenzied activity ceases abruptly. The dynamic level drops, there is a brief reference to the material of the introductory paragraph and the final line of the text – 'And trust to the immaculate blood to wash thy score', which is brought forward a little from its actual position in Donne's poem – is sung *pianissimo*, as if in complete exhaustion after the previous overwrought, emotional outpouring. Thus, in masterly fashion, she succeeds in conveying the poet's sudden, shocked realisation that given true faith, such terrifying anguish is needless. The vocal line falls to the F-sharp on which it began; the tonality is finally confirmed as modal (which throughout Ina Boyle's work seems to function as a kind of tonal symbol for untroubled acceptance and trust); and the work ends in quiet confidence on a peaceful F-sharp major chord.

Of Ina Boyle's five compositions for solo voice and orchestra by far the most ambitious is Symphony No. 3, *From the Darkness*, which she completed in 1951, having worked on it for over five years. In this work Boyle has attempted one of the most difficult of sub-genres, the song-symphony, an extended composition for solo voice (or voices) and orchestra the textures and proportions of which are of sufficient complexity and on large enough a scale to justify the description 'symphonic'. The song-symphony is a very different kind of work to the song cycle with orchestra where, however diverse the individual forms – from strophic to through-composed – and however ingenious their inter-relationships, the component items remain identifiably songs in weight and in dimensions. One thinks, for example, of a work like Edward Elgar's *Sea Pictures*, Op. 37 (1899), on the one hand, which has five discrete, fairly straightforward songs, or Benjamin Britten's *Nocturne*, Op. 60 (1958), on the other, which has eight subtly interconnected numbers. In the song-symphony, however, the accent falls firmly on the word 'symphony', which always entails far more than a vocal line with a supporting accompaniment, however sophisticated the compositional technique may be. The term implies not merely the presentation of appropriately varied thematic material but also, and crucially, the way this material is treated and developed. This in turn implies an expansion of the time-scale of the constituent settings, which now perforce become symphonic movements. The integration of a solo vocal line into complex, developmental procedures, and in a manner that is consistent with a natural response to the sung text, presents the composer with considerable technical challenges.

Few have in fact chosen to grapple with these challenges. There are, of course, symphonies in which the solo voice is featured as an extension of the expressive resource of the orchestra – as in *A Pastoral Symphony* by Vaughan Williams (soprano solo), for example, or Nielsen's Symphony No. 3, *Sinfonia Espansiva* (soprano and baritone soli), where it is employed wordlessly, almost as an additional instrument; and there are symphonies in which one of the movements is cast as a song, such as Mahler's Symphony No. 4. But there are very few in which the solo voice is an integral part of the entire conception. Even Mahler's *Das Lied von der Erde*, considered by many to be a symphony in all but name, has many obvious points of contact with the song cycle, the large dimensions, especially of the final movement, notwithstanding.

From the Darkness is therefore a very rare example of a full-scale, three-movement symphony in which a solo voice (contralto in this case) is not only absolutely central to the idea of the work, but around which each of the three movements is designed. The nearest contemporary example of this extensive employment of a solo voice in a symphony (also, as it happens, a contralto) is perhaps Karl Amadeus Hartmann's Symphony No. 1, *Versuch eines Requiem*. The first version of Hartmann's symphony was performed in 1948, after which it was revised by the composer and not performed again until 1957. It is very unlikely that Ina Boyle knew of it. Hartmann's texts are chosen from a German translation of Walt Whitman, but, unlike Boyle's work, not all the movements feature the soloist: the central movement of the five that make up the symphony is a purely orchestral theme and variations.

For the texts of *From the Darkness*, Boyle turned once again to her close contemporary, the English poet Edith Sitwell (1887–1964). Sitwell's reputation as a poet was at its height during the years of the Second World War, when she produced some of her most memorable verse. Boyle chose three poems from this period, which she may well have encountered as they first appeared either in the literary periodicals of the day or in the *Times Literary Supplement*.[36] The first movement is a setting of a poem called 'Invocation', which Sitwell subsequently included in *Green Song and Other Poems* (1944); the second and third movements are based on two poems that were published in a volume entitled *Street Songs* (1942), 'An Old Woman' and 'Harvest' respectively.[37]

However Boyle may have first come across these three poems, she showed a keen literary perceptiveness in bringing them together as the basis of her symphony. They are intimately connected, not only through the persona of the narrating voice – 'I, an old woman' – but also through a similarity of tone and of poetic imagery. When she came to publish her *Collected Poems* in 1957, Sitwell, too, placed the three poems together and, interestingly, in the same order in which they appear in *From the Darkness*. As well as their general thematic outlook, the technical suitability of the poems for symphonic treatment also testifies to considerable compositional acuity. They are written in free verse – irregular lines grouped into stanzas of varying length – and Sitwell's eschewal of metrical regularity or recurring stanza forms necessitates a complex musical response. From the composer's point of view, the choice of a straightforward, regularly constructed poem may lead either to the composition of a more or less straightforward song or, if the obvious design of the poem is deliberately contradicted, to the risk of self-conscious preciousness. The very incompatibility of these Sitwell texts with simple song-like treatment is exactly what is needed for the kind of work Boyle had in mind. (It is interesting to note that, in selecting passages from Whitman for his Symphony No. 1, Hartmann chose a very similar kind of text.)

At her finest, Edith Sitwell is primarily a religious poet, and the intensity of her vision is conveyed in a hieratic, incantatory style. The first poem, 'Invocation', is a prayer for light in a time of darkness; in the dead of winter the poet patiently awaits the renewal of spring. In the second poem, 'An Old Woman', the waiting continues, but the tone is now serenely confident – 'Wise is the earth, consoling grief and glory' – and it rises to a magnificent climax:

> For though the soundless wrinkles fall like snow
> On many a golden cheek, and creeds grow old
> And change, – man's heart, that sun,
> Outlives all terrors shaking the old night:
> The world's huge fevers burn and shine, turn cold,
> Yet the heavenly bodies and young lovers burn and shine,
> The golden lovers walk in the holy fields
> Where the Abraham-bearded sun, the father of all things,
> Is shouting of ripeness, and the whole world of dews and
>   splendours are singing
> To the cradles of earth, of men, beasts, harvests, swinging
> In the peace of God's heart.

The mood of the final poem, 'Harvest', is one of fulfilment – 'O sons of men, the firmament's belovèd / The Golden Ones of heaven have us in care' – a mystical vision in which nature imagery and images from Christian theology are bound together into an ecstatic paean. In the final lines, in an evocation of the harvest, of the Last Supper and the Christian Sacrament of Communion, the crops of golden wheat become the Seraphim, who, in the 'universal language of the Bread'

> Roar from the Earth: 'Our Christ is arisen, He comes to
> give a sign from the Dead'.

This is poetry that gains immeasurably by being read aloud (and Sitwell was an impressive reader of her own work). By extension, it is also poetry that accommodates itself well to being sung, especially when the setting is careful to project the feeling of incantation and is able to heighten into specific pitches the declamatory quality of the verse, while at the same time preserving its rhythmic freedom.

Boyle's response to the challenging task that she set herself is remarkably assured. Her approach to the setting of the words is to evolve a free arioso line for the soloist. The settings are by and large syllabic, although expressive melismas are employed at moments of particular emotional intensity, and the lines move easily and naturally between simple recitative, on the one hand, and more broadly expansive contours, on the other. Apart from one or two moments, the vocal line scarcely refers to the thematic content of the symphony, but this independence does not mean that the vocal part is unrelated to the symphonic unfolding that takes place in the orchestra. On the contrary, the thematic content of the work, its organisation and its development is designed to be both a complement to and a consequence of the vocal line, but more to the psychological import of the words than to the precise musical content of the arioso. In addition, the thematic material of the symphony is cleverly and imaginatively conceived so that it can command the foreground when necessary, but also retire unobtrusively into the background whenever the voice needs to move into prominence. By the 1940s, Boyle's characteristic approach of deriving the substance of the music from internally developing thematic material had become quite sophisticated, and it proved to be the ideal technique for the present work. The fabric of the symphony, in other words, is permeated by ever-evolving, ever-developing ideas that obviate the need for 'development sections' as such and allow standard sonata-form procedures – which are notoriously difficult to reconcile with setting a text – to be set aside, but without at the same time compromising the symphonic potential of the music.

Each of the poems that Boyle chose is quite lengthy, and in order to create a settable text of manageable proportions she had of necessity to cut them fairly substantially. Although undoubtedly it would not have pleased the poet, it has to be acknowledged that she has done this with considerable literary tact and succeeded well in preserving the essential import of Sitwell's work.

The first movement, 'Invocation', is in a modal B minor (which may be regarded as the prevailing tonality of the symphony as a whole) and the tempo (*Grave*) remains slow throughout. It starts with an introduction in which the poetic persona announces herself and establishes the psychological perspective from which the entire symphony takes its point of departure (Ex. 37):

> I who was once a golden woman like those who walk
> In the dark heavens – but am now grown old
> And sit by the fire, and see the fire grow cold,
> Watch the dark fields for a rebirth of faith and wonder.

Ex. 37: Symphony No. 3, *From the Darkness*, I, bars 1–8

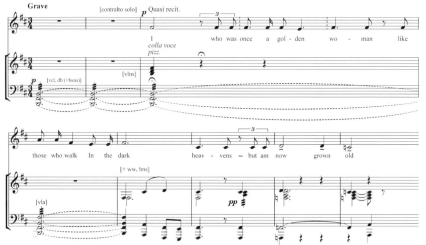

At the word 'wonder', the end of the introduction overlaps with the beginning of the movement proper, marked *Più lento*. This is cast in what might be described as rondo form – A-B-A¹-C-A² – where each of the component sections not only presents but also develops significant thematic material, an ongoing process that is also applied to the material of the opening section as it returns.

Ex. 38: Symphony No. 3, *From the Darkness*, I, bars 16–27

The A section commences with a long paragraph for orchestra alone which is based on a yearning, chromatically inflected theme (Ex. 38) to which the high string writing (particularly for the cellos and violas) imparts a quality of almost painful intensity. This culminates in the re-entry of the solo voice with the words 'And speaking of love are the voices that come from the darkness', at which point we hear a new motif on solo oboe which remains associated with the idea of love throughout the movement (Ex. 39). Both of these themes, together with some subsidiary material, are then developed in tandem until the passionate outburst of the soloist at the beginning of the second section, B – 'O Love, return to the dying world' – is articulated by a group of new ideas (Ex. 40). The mood has changed and the music has acquired a new urgency as the soloist now embarks on a direct, pleading address to Love. Interestingly, the A¹ section that ensues reverses the original order of the material and, as the music regains a measure of calm, Ex. 39 (still on oboe solo) accompanies the line 'Be then [still addressing Love, presumably] the spirit working in the dark earth'.[38] All the principal ideas of A (together with stray echoes of B) are subject to continuous reworking throughout this section and the initial feeling of calm gives way to a more unsettled atmosphere. No real sense of tranquillity is regained until the commencement of section C, where the idea of peace is, in

Ex. 39: Symphony No. 3, *From the Darkness*, I, bars 41–42

Ex. 40: Symphony No. 3, *From the Darkness*, I, 63–69

fact, explicitly invoked in the text – 'but in the night / The Holy Ghost speaks in the whispering leaves'. This sense of quietude is carried through into the final section, A², and the movement ends movingly on B major harmony with a hushed prayer for the redemption of mankind: 'and wash the stain / From the darkened hands of the universal Cain'.

The flowing six-eight *Allegretto tranquillo* of the second movement, 'An Old Woman', provides an excellent contrast to the uniformly slow pace of 'Invocation'. It, too, is constructed as a rondo – A-B-A¹-C-A² – this time, however, without any introduction. The opening A section, in G major, is the nearest thing in the symphony to straightforward song-like writing, where the principal melodic interest is carried by the soloist and the orchestra provides an accompaniment (Ex. 41). This relatively simple approach is not maintained throughout, however, and the textures become more complex as the ideas are subject to development.

After 'Still Falls the Rain', 'An Old Woman' is arguably the most famous poem Sitwell composed during the war years. While it would be a mistake naively to identify the poetic persona of the old woman with Sitwell herself (or indeed, by extension, with Ina Boyle), it presents a rare state of mind in which hardship and suffering can be transcended, understanding attained, and forgiveness eventually made possible. Given the time of its composition, it is a remarkably positive utterance and its unshakable assurance made a deep impression when it was first published. Despite the convulsions mankind was experiencing at the time, it radiates confidence that there are certainties, spiritual certainties, that are deep and unchanging, 'swinging / In the peace of God's heart'.

Ex. 41: Symphony No. 3, *From the Darkness*, II, 1–8

In its own quiet way – for the music rarely rises above *mezzo forte* – Boyle's response is equally affirmative. The A section gives way to the first episode, B. Here the soloist describes 'the evenings bringing home the workers', and although the murmuring semiquavers of the prevailing six-eight are maintained, the tonality is suitably darkened (B-flat major) to register the change of mood. With the onset of the A[1] section the tonality again brightens, but this yields quickly to the second episode, C, which is radically different from what has gone before. The tempo increases to *più animato*, the time signature to five-four and the tonality shifts mysteriously from the prevailing G major to a modal F minor. This is in preparation for the setting of the passage commencing 'Wise is the earth', and it incorporates the climactic lines quoted above. There is a transition passage in preparation for the final return of the opening material, A[2], in which the six-eight time is restored and G major is regained as the line 'swinging / In the peace of God's heart' is sung (the arrival of the chord of G major is precisely timed to coincide with the word 'peace'). It is an unusual moment, because, although it is undoubtedly the goal of the movement, the dynamic level is *pianissimo* and it is approached from a *diminuendo*, all of which seem to convey the feeling that such spiritual certainty does not need to be shouted aloud.

The prevailing modal B minor returns for the finale, 'Harvest', which, like the first movement, begins with a slow introduction. In its general organisation, this is the movement in which Boyle comes closest to a sonata-type disposition of the materials: A-B-C-A^1-B^1/coda, where C is an independent episode and the abbreviated B^1 is transmuted into a coda. In practice, however, the technical approach is the same as in the earlier movements. Although there is some thematic cross-referencing, particularly at the end, the individual sections develop their own distinctive material internally, and are thus constructed in a comparable way to the component sections of the previous two movements.

Ex. 42: Symphony No. 3, *From the Darkness*, III, bars 13–25

After the *Lento* introduction, the tempo increases to an *Allegro* that is maintained throughout the finale. Not only is this, therefore, a very welcome span of fast music, but it also represents an acceleration of tempo across the three movements of the symphony that is clearly intended to correspond to the overall psychological trajectory of the three Sitwell poems. The A section begins with an urgent rising, dotted idea which is dispersed in animated semiquaver figuration that prepares for the soloist's entry, 'We asked for a sign that we have not been forsaken' (Ex. 42). These ideas (along with some subsidiary material) are developed at some length and lead directly to the B section (*Più tranquillo*). Here the semiquaver movement is maintained, but now it moves into the background as a murmuring accompaniment to the passage commencing 'O sons of men, the firmament's belovèd'. This is one of the few moments in the work when contour of the vocal line assumes a distinct thematic profile that will re-emerge significantly later in the movement. The central C section is not long, and although it has its own distinct textural and thematic identity at the outset, it acquires some of the characteristics of a genuine development section as material from A (not so much the characteristic dotted idea which is held in reserve, but the subsidiary material) is worked up into a climax. This leads inevitably to the return of the principal opening ideas, A¹. The brief reference to the secondary section (B¹), now in a limpid B major, is confined to the fragment of the vocal line heard earlier, which is transferred to the violins in a moment of radiant illumination as the words 'The Seraphim rank on rank of ripe wheat' are sung. The remainder of the movement (at once the coda and the psychological climax of the symphony as a whole) is based on material from A, and after the soloist has delivered the final ecstatic lines (quoted above), the music dies away, ending the work as it began, quietly, on a tonally ambiguous open fifth – B-F-sharp – in the low strings.

From the Darkness is unquestionably one of Ina Boyle's most important works. Under what circumstances she envisaged its performance is not known (conditions in Ireland at the time were certainly not propitious for the performance of new symphonies by native composers). Whatever she may have hoped for, her disappointment must have been acute when Edith Sitwell's refusal of permission to use her poems effectively stifled the work at birth.

The last major creative project that Ina Boyle undertook was the composition of a chamber opera, which occupied her for several years and which was finally completed in 1964. Although it appears that she wrote it for her own amusement and had little or no expectation that it would ever be staged, the work was nonetheless brought to a highly finished state. Not only is there a complete orchestral score amongst her papers – which is precisely and meticulously edited – but she also left a vocal score that is clearly designed for rehearsal purposes. Composing the opera may have been an exercise in the creation of a private imaginative world, but there was nothing vague about it. The work is thoroughly realised in every detail, not merely musically, but right down to suggestions for the costumes and sketches for the stage sets. It is difficult to believe that somewhere at the back of her mind there did not lurk a faint hope that someday it might be performed, although the prospect of a new opera by a native Irish composer being staged in the Ireland of the 1960s was virtually non-existent, and is something that remains slim even today.

Unfortunately, however, *Maudlin of Paplewick* is problematic in several respects, and it is unlikely that it would ever be considered stageworthy. One hesitates, therefore, to discuss it in detail, not merely because its defects must inevitably prompt a response that may seem unduly negative, but also because the very private and personal circumstances of its composition might make this criticism seem both insensitive and impertinent. On the other hand, to omit it altogether from the discussion of her music would be to present a distorted picture of Boyle's achievements; flawed though it may be, it is nonetheless an important and significant work in the context of her output.

The libretto is an adaptation, amounting to little more than an abridgement, by Boyle herself of *The Sad Shepherd, or a Tale of Robin Hood*, an unfinished pastoral play by Ben Jonson (1572–1637) that probably dates from the last year of his life, and that features Robin Hood, Maid Marian, Friar Tuck and other traditionally associated characters.[39] Jonson's text is largely retained intact: there are a few cuts – two minor characters have been eliminated – the speeches are trimmed a little, and there is some transposition and rearrangement of the material. Otherwise, the libretto adheres fairly closely to the order of the action in the play.

What survives of *The Sad Shepherd* comprises the first two acts and a portion of the third act. On the assumption that, like Jonson's other plays, it would if completed have been in five acts, this suggests that only about half of the projected play exists. We have no idea how it might have ended, or of how the various strands of the plot might ultimately have been worked out. To the composer, therefore, falls the difficult task of supplying a plausible conclusion while at the same time remaining faithful both to Jonson's dramatic conception and to the poetic atmosphere he creates.

Act I is set in Robin Hood's bower in Sherwood Forest, and the curtain rises to reveal Aeglamour, the eponymous Sad Shepherd of Jonson's play. He passes dejectedly across the scene, and from the exaggeratedly mournful manner in which he talks about his beloved we gather that something is amiss. He wanders off distractedly, and Maid Marian enters with several companions, including Friar Tuck and Little John. They discuss Robin Hood's recent absence and how he is expected back in Sherwood that very day. Robin has already conveyed his intention of hosting an entertainment for all the shepherds, and Marian is on the point of setting off for the hunt as he has asked her to provide venison for the feast. As she leaves, Aeglamour reappears saying that he believes his beloved, Earine, has been drowned in the River Trent. He blames her death on the carelessness of his fellow shepherds and in his distraught state of mind he talks wildly of revenge. Robin arrives and Aeglamour, who is sitting apart from the others in a state of distress, is pointed out to him, but neither his sympathy nor a sad song about love and death sung by Karolin, Earine's brother, can console the unhappy shepherd. Back from the chase, Marian greets Robin Hood lovingly, and amid kisses and endearments tells him of her successful expedition before departing to the kitchen to inspect the venison.

Up to this point, the opera's title character, Maudlin of Paplewick, has only been mentioned in passing. But we have learned that she is a witch and that it was she who first told Aeglamour that Earine had been drowned. We also hear that she is adept at shape-shifting and that Marian's huntsman believes a large, ominous-looking raven seen at the kill was none other than Maudlin herself. When, presently, Maid Marian re-enters she is startlingly altered in her demeanour. Now no longer warm and loving, she is shrill and shrewish and she orders that the venison she has just brought home be sent as a gift to Maudlin of Paplewick. Robin, astonished by this sudden change, can hardly believe his ears and as Act I closes he determines to discover what is behind it. This strong conclusion to the act is unfortunately weakened by Boyle who, instead of allowing Robin to exit, keeps him on stage while Little John sings a song, 'In summer when the shaws be sheen', to words which she imports into the play. Although Boyle is careful to avoid any poetic incongruity – the words are chosen from what is thought to be the oldest existing ballad about Robin Hood, *Robin Hood and the Monk*, which dates from about the middle of the fifteenth century[40] – the decision to postpone the first act curtain for a superfluous lyrical insertion is undoubtedly a dramatic miscalculation.

The setting for Act II is another part of the forest showing the dimble, or hollow, where Maudlin lives. The witch gloats triumphantly over her successful impersonation of Maid Marian – thus explaining the recent apparent change in Marian's behaviour – and she boasts that by this means she will sow the seeds of bitter discord between her and Robin Hood. Maudlin, too, we discover, is responsible for the disappearance of Earine. Her supposed drowning was staged by the witch, who abducted her as a mate – willing or unwilling as the case may be – for her uncouth son, Lorel. Having temporarily released her from the oak tree in which she is now imprisoned, Lorel duly attempts to woo her, but Earine is merely horrified and repulses him in disgust. Out of a desire to cause further confusion, Maudlin dresses Douce, her daughter, in Earine's garments and sends her to mingle with the shepherds. The act ends with the appearance of Puck – in a scene transposed from the beginning of Act III of the play – who explains that although Maudlin 'grows high in evil' she could do little without his supernatural assistance.

Boyle decided to hold over the second scene of Act II of the play to become the opening of Act III of the opera. The setting is the same as in Act I. Robin Hood reproaches Maid Marian with her strange behaviour which, being innocent, she naturally disavows. She is amazed to hear that, apparently at her own behest, the venison has been sent to Maudlin and she immediately orders its retrieval. Maudlin then enters and brazenly proceeds to thank Marian for her thoughtful gift. Marian disabuses her, and as the recovered venison is brought in Maudlin becomes threatening and begins to mutter curses under her breath. (These are directed at the cook who, as we eventually learn, is afflicted with sudden cramps and pains in the course of preparing the venison.) In a secondary thread of the plot, Amie, sister to Lionel, has become innocently enamoured of Karolin. She is lovesick to the point of causing concern and Marian asks that Karolin be sent for in the hope that his presence might help cure her. Maudlin overhears these arrangements being made just as she is about to take her leave, and malignantly she vows to keep Amie and Karolin apart. It now becomes clear to Robin that Maid Marian must surely have been impersonated by the shape-shifting witch and on the advice of Alken, a wise old shepherd, he decides that she must be pursued and apprehended.

Maudlin's daughter enters dressed as Earine. She encounters Karolin, and is also seen by Aeglamour who, now quite deranged with grief, imagines she is the ghost of his beloved and that she is communing with the planetary spheres. Just as Lionel is explaining to Karolin that Amie loves him, Maudlin enters, having once again assumed Marian's outward appearance, and tells them that in point of fact Amie has quite recovered and that Karolin is not needed. Robin chances upon the scene and recognises the transformed Maudlin for who she really is. He challenges her and in the ensuing tussle removes her magic girdle, whereupon she reverts to her own shape. Remaining at a safe distance, she demands the return of the girdle, but Robin refuses and tells her he has given orders for her to be hunted down. She calls on Puck for assistance and, as he advises her how she might best evade her enemies, Lorel enters on his way to renew his wooing of Earine.

It is at this point that Ben Jonson's play breaks off. Every single thread of the story is thus left hanging loosely. Not only is there no indication of what the intended outcome may have been, but because of the incompleteness of the play, several of the characters, as well as the events in which they take part, remain without ultimate dramatic justification. Jonson may have had a clear idea how the various strands were to be drawn together; we, however, can only guess how this might have been accomplished.

In attempting to turn *The Sad Shepherd* into an opera, therefore, Ina Boyle was faced with two separate but related challenges: first, to develop the various strands of Jonson's plot and bring them to a satisfactory conclusion; and second, to determine the manner in which this should be done. Given the unlikelihood of being able to provide two and a half additional acts of pastiche Jonson, both of these questions might more feasibly have been addressed if, instead of deciding to set the play more or less as it stood, Boyle had been prepared to consider it as a point of departure for an entirely new libretto in modern English. But she clearly never entertained this as a possibility. Indeed, one suspects that apart from the pastoral setting, which seems to have had a particular appeal for her, it was the rich texture and vivid imagery of Jonson's blank verse that attracted her to the play in the first place. While understandable, this in itself created difficulties. The primary function of a libretto, after all, is to create a dramatic structure that provides suitable opportunities for music, and fine poetry does not necessarily facilitate this. In *The Sad Shepherd*, the text frequently blossoms into substantial, poetically evocative speeches for the characters, which may be effective in a spoken play, but in an opera merely obstruct the full *musical* realisation of the dramatic situations as they unfold. In other words, and speaking generally, the verbal aspect of the drama must be dissolved before it can be satisfactorily reconstituted into the primarily musical aspect of the opera. This is not to say that plays conceived and constructed in a manner that makes them suitable for operatic treatment, either as they stand or with minimal alteration, do not exist – they do, and composers have set them – but *The Sad Shepherd* is not, I think, amongst them.[41] If it was unthinkable for Boyle that the story might be filled out with words not written by Jonson, the price she paid was to lumber herself with a fairly intractable text, on the one hand, and an insoluble problem of what to do about the ending, on the other.

As a preface to the play, Jonson provided a summary, or argument, for the first three acts in which the continuation of Act III is outlined beyond what was actually written. Boyle availed of this to sidestep the double question of how the plot might be developed and the manner in which it might be done. Based on the summary, she devised a pantomime in which the characters act out to accompanying music what she decided would suffice as the concluding events of the story: Earine is freed and restored to Aeglamour, Maudlin is pursued but ultimately escapes, and so on. Apart from the fact that this represents merely an interim situation in the play as conceived by Jonson, not an ending, and that it entails inevitable dramatic inconsequentialities, it is hardly a convincing solution.[42] For one thing, the amount of space devoted to the exposition of events is completely disproportionate to that allotted to their outcome: out of a full score of 622 pages, the final pantomime occupies a mere thirty-three. As a conclusion, it is perfunctory. But, more importantly, to present the entire denouement of an opera without the participation of the singing voice – or even, as a substitute, the speaking voice – must result in an anti-climax. Boyle understood that she could not actually bring down the curtain without the resumption of singing, so she appended two further items after the pantomime: a solo song for Maid Marian, 'Now sleep, and take thy rest', which is addressed to Aeglamour; and arising out of it, a concluding ensemble (a septet) for the principal characters, 'Worship, O ye that lovers be this May'. Again, as in the case of the addition to the end of Act I, Boyle gave careful consideration to the choice of words: the text of the first is a translation from the Spanish by James Mabbe, a contemporary of Jonson's, and that of the second is a modernised extract from a much earlier work, *The Kingis Quair* by King James I of Scotland.[43] These importations, however, amount to little more than a final flourish and they add nothing essential to the drama. After the septet, the board is prepared for the feast and, as the on-stage musicians welcome the arriving guests, the curtain comes down on a cheerfully festive scene.[44]

Given the inherent disadvantages, it is puzzling why Ina Boyle chose to base her opera on this particular play. It seems that she simply did not have sufficient experience to assess the appeal of the theme and the rich suggestiveness of Jonson's poetry in relation to its overall theatrical viability, failing even to appreciate how eighteen singing roles (together with extras) might militate against the possibility of performance. It may be, of course, that she was well aware of these shortcomings but chose to ignore them; after all, the size of the cast is scarcely relevant in an opera conceived for performance only in the imagination of the composer. This brings us to the contradiction at the heart of *Maudlin of Paplewick*: a fundamentally impractical conception is realised in a score that has been meticulously completed and presented so as to ensure its absolute feasibility for musical performance. Perhaps it was because she had become so accustomed to working in isolation that it never seems to have occurred to her to consult someone more experienced in the theatre who might have been able to advise her about what would or would not be effective on the stage, and one assumes that theatrical effectiveness, at least theoretically, was something she hoped to achieve.

Musically speaking, the score is very deftly written. Because Boyle put herself in the position of having to dispatch a great deal of text, her principal approach to setting the words is to adopt a free, flexible melodic style in which the rhythms and pitch contours can convey in an easy, fluent manner the emotional rise and fall of the verse. The benefit of this technique is that it can embrace both recitative and arioso as necessary, fluctuating smoothly between dry, rapid delivery and more sustained lyrical passages, while at the same time ensuring the efficient forward movement of the plot. Boyle's extensive reliance on it, however, means that her score lacks the emotional and psychological focus that full-blown set-pieces – arias, duets and so on – were conceived to supply. It is in these moments of expanded feeling that the inner life of the characters is revealed. Without them, or without their more sophisticated substitutes as evolved by Wagner or Puccini, an operatic score will inevitably remain somewhat one-dimensional. Given the undiluted diatonic idiom and restrained pastoral manner of *Maudlin of Paplewick*, stylised folk-song would probably have sufficed in place of the aria, but the same principle obtains, even if functioning at a lower emotional level. The structure of the opera's individual scenes, therefore, is largely independent of the content of the vocal lines. Instead, by developing characteristic instrumental patterns and succinct melodic or motivic ideas into continuously evolving background textures, Boyle aims to make the accompaniment the principal agent of formal coherence and the skill with which she brings this off makes it one of the most conspicuously successful aspects of the score. In terms of balance and contrast, the succession of different textures as one scene moves into the next is managed with great naturalness: the tempi are well judged as are the tonalities, and the whole is supported by an imaginative handling of the chamber orchestra for which Boyle scored the work, and from which she extracts a great deal of colour and variety.[45]

For Boyle, *Maudlin of Paplewick* was 'a kind of children's opera', as she somewhat tentatively put it: not an opera to be performed by children – it is technically much too demanding for that – but presumably an opera to be performed for the entertainment of children. Even here her inexperience is apparent, however. Although the work is certainly unpretentious, she seems not to have understood that children require music they can easily grasp, usually in the form of straightforward melodies and simple, clear-cut structures, something the subtle elusiveness of her compositional approach precluded. Unfortunately, the way the music is conceived also means that the score does not facilitate the extraction of discrete numbers: songs (or arias), choruses, instrumental interludes and so on. This is a pity, because, given the fact the opera is unlikely ever to reach the stage, the only way some at least of the music might have been heard would have been in the form of detachable extracts, but virtually none of it – and this is true even of the imported songs – is viable outside its immediate dramatic context. *Maudlin of Paplewick*, it would seem, is destined to remain a silent monument to the ceaseless, dedicated but essentially private creative activity of Ina Boyle's final years.

At present, Ina Boyle's exact place in the history of Irish music remains unclear: too little of her music has been performed for any confident final assessment to be made of her overall achievement, and the works that have succeeded in attracting attention are, unfortunately, not always representative of her best. From the general cultural point of view, her outlook was what might be expected from someone of her Protestant Anglo-Irish background – focused primarily on England and London – and she never seems to have considered that as a composer she might have a part to play in articulating the new Ireland that was struggling into existence in the early decades of the twentieth century. Her decision to set Herbert Asquith's elegiac sonnet in 1916, with its reference to the fallen soldiers who are 'graven deep in England's memory', and her silence about the cataclysmic events that were taking place on her doorstep in Dublin, speaks for itself. This outlook is reflected in the literature to which she turned for inspiration and which, no doubt, she would unselfconsciously have regarded as the natural reading material of generally cultured people: English literature mostly, with a smattering of Greek and Latin classics in translation. She did occasionally set the work of Irish poets writing in English – she does not appear to have had any interest in Gaelic culture or any knowledge of the Irish language – and there are songs with words by George Russell, James Stephens, Austin Clarke and a few others; she even set one or two translations from the Irish. But this is scarcely more than one might find in the work of any English songwriter who was reasonably well read in contemporary lyric poetry. The modal idiom of her music is not the result of any personal study of folk music, and certainly not of Irish folk music. It appears to have arisen quite naturally and spontaneously out of a desire to develop an individual voice by sidestepping the more obvious procedures of standard nineteenth-century tonal practice, an approach she shared with many of her contemporaries, both in England and elsewhere. If its contours and turns of phrase suggest the influence of folk song at all, this is likely to have been filtered through the work of English figures like Vaughan Williams.

This aloofness, or perhaps just simply remoteness, from the cultural ferment of early twentieth-century Ireland set her apart, to a degree, from many of her contemporaries. One only has to think of how, in the wake of the Irish Literary Renaissance and the Gaelic Revival, successive figures like Carl Hardebeck (1869–1945), John F. Larchet (1884–1967), Éamon Ó Gallchobhair (1906–1982), Aloys Fleischmann (1910–1992) and others were attempting to contribute to the creation of a distinctive Irish art music. Even the music of Charles Villiers Stanford (1852–1924) and Hamilton Harty (1879–1941), whose careers were based entirely in Britain, reflects their Irish backgrounds to a greater degree than Boyle's does. This is not to suggest that the music itself is necessarily any the worse for this, but it does mean that there is a danger of her being evaluated as a mere cross-channel epigone of the English musical renaissance, which would be unjust.

She is the only resident Irish composer to have produced a series of major scores here during the 1920s and, even more remarkably, she is the only native Irish composer to have written full-scale orchestral symphonies between Stanford's Symphony No. 7 of 1911 and Seóirse Bodley's Symphony No. 1 of 1959.[46] This fact alone would earn her a special place in the history of Irish composition. In Symphony No. 1, *'Glencree' (In the Wicklow Hills)*, she is clearly finding her feet as a symphonic composer, and while the score is not without interest, it has a number of obvious shortcomings. However, her achievement both in Symphony No. 2, *The Dream of the Rood*, and in Symphony No. 3, *From the Darkness*, is on a different level. *From the Darkness* in particular is an extraordinary work from many points of view, not least in that it unites into a single moving utterance the work of two strong, independent-minded women who were in some respects very different – Edith Sitwell, the acclaimed English poet on the one hand, and on the other, the largely unknown Irish composer, living in isolation and working in obscurity – but whose shared sense of unchanging spiritual certainties vouchsafed them a vision of hope in a time of despair. Sitwell's serene imperturbability during the war years in London was legendary, but in sheer resilience and quiet determination Ina Boyle was every bit the equal of the formidable author of her chosen texts, something the very story of her career as described in this volume surely demonstrates. As a symphony for solo voice and orchestra, *From the Darkness* is impressive both in the manner of its conception and of its realisation. In the context of Irish music it is unique. Both it and the earlier *Dream of the Rood* – not to mention many of her other pieces – undoubtedly merit being rescued from the oblivion in which they have languished for so many years. While a serious critical re-evaluation of her creative achievement has long been overdue, it is only committed, sympathetic performances of her music that can truly reveal Ina Boyle as a composer of greater range and significance than has hitherto been imagined, and establish her rightful place in the history of Irish music.

Leabharlanna Poiblí Chathair Baile Átha Cliath

Dublin City Public Libraries

APPENDIX I

Genealogy

CRAMPTON

1   Sir Philip Crampton Bart. MD FRCS, created baronet 1839 (b. 7 June 1777, d. 10 June 1858), m. 12 May 1802 Selina Cannon (b. 1781, d. 1834), 3 sons, 4 daughters

1.1 Sir John Fiennes Twisleton Crampton Bart. KCB (b. 13 August 1805, d. 5 Dec. 1886), m. 31 March 1860 Victoire Balfe (b. 1837, d. 1871), marriage dissolved 1863

1.2 Anna Maria (Philly) Crampton (b. 1807, d. December 1886), m. Eugene Le Clerc (d. 1884), Surgeon to Constabulary Depot, Phoenix Park

1.3 Rev. Josiah Crampton (b. 1809, d. Great Sutton, Essex, 8 March 1883), m. 1833 Elizabeth Crampton, 8 daughters

1.4 Selina Crampton (b. 15 August 1811, d. 5 January 1893)

1.5 Charlotte Crampton (b. 1 March 1813, d. 24 october 1869)

1.6 Adelaide Crampton (b. 13 June 1816, d. 15 April 1892), m. 1840 Captain Henry Prittie George Jephson, 87th Royal Irish Fusiliers (b. 13 June 1813, d. 31 March 1866), 1 son 3 daughters [*see 2 below*]

1.7 Philip Crampton (b.?, d. 16 May 1813)

JEPHSON

2   Captain Henry Prittie George Jephson 87th Royal Irish Fusiliers (b. 1813, d. 31 March 1866), m. 1840 Adelaide Crampton (b. 13 June 1816, d. 15 April 1892), 1 son, 3 daughters

2.1 Selina Martha Jephson (b. 1841), m. 1859 Richars Carey Elwes (b. 1827)

2.2 Henry Lorenzo Jephson J.P. (b. 1845, d. London, 31 January 1914), 1 son, 2 daughters [*see 3 below*]

2.3 Adelaide Elizabeth Jephson (b. 24 January 1850, d. 29 June 1880), m. 26 March 1874 Captain Wills-Sandford, Royal Scots Greys (b. 12 April 1844, d. 3 April 1889), 1 son, 2 daughters [*see 4 below*]

2.4 Philippa Arabella Jephson (b. 17 April 1857, d. 9 April 1932), m. May 1882 Rev. W. F. Boyle MA (b. 5 September 1860, d. 14 November 1951), 2 daughters [*see 5 below*]

3   Henry Lorenzo Jephson J.P. (b. 1845, d. London, 31 January 1914), 1 son, 2 daughters
3.1 Major Philip Henry Jephson OBE (b. Middlesex, 1 February 1888)
3.2 Adelaide Jephson (d. London, 1977), m. Captain Grenville Fortescue (b. 15 March 1887, d. 4 September 1915), 1 son, 1 daughter [*see 6 below*]. Married 10 March 1930 Brigadier Robin Leslie Hutchins, 2 sons, 1 daughter
3.3 Ina (Selina) Jephson (d. London, 1 October 1961)

WILLS-SANDFORD
4   Captain William Robert Wills-Sandford, Royal Scots Greys (b. 12 April 1844, d. 3 April 1889), m. 26 March 1874 Adelaide Elizabeth Jephson (b. 24 January 1850, d. 29 June 1880), 1 son, 2 daughters
4.1 Charlotte Georgina Wills-Sandford (b. 25 July 1875, d. 20 May 1940), m. Charles Wood (b. 15 June 1866, d. 12 July 1926), 2 sons, 3 daughters [*see 7 below*]
4.2 Mary Adelaide Wills-Sandford (b. 29 September 1877, d. 23 January 1956)
4.3 Thomas George Wills-Sandford (b. 9 November 1879, d. 10 May 1948)

BOYLE
5   Rev. William Foster Boyle MA (b. 5 September 1860, d. 14 November 1951), m. May 1887 Philippa Arabella Jephson (b. 17 April 1857, d. 9 April 1932), 2 daughters
5.1 Selina Adelaide Philippa Boyle (b. 8 March 1889, d. 10 March 1967)
5.2 Phyllis Kathleen Boyle (b. 6 July 1890, d. 21 July 1938)

FORTESCUE
6   Captain Grenville Fortescue (b. 15 March 1887, d. 4 September 1915), m. Adelaide Jephson, 1 son, 1 daughter
6.1 Fortescue Brigadier Arthur Henry Grenville MC, MBE (b. 6 September 1913, d. 8 Feb. 2005), m. 30 April 1946 Rosita Campbell, 2 sons
6.2 Diana Fortescue (b. 2 January 1915, d. 13 May 2009), m. 1945 Lt. Colonel Charles Floyd OBE, marriage dissolved 1947

WOOD
7   Charles Wood (b. 15 June 1866, d. 12 July 1926), m. Charlotte Wills-Sandford (b. 25 July 1875, d. 20 May 1940), 2 sons, 3 daughters
7.1 Bryan Wood (b. 1899, d. 1918)
7.2 Edward Mathew Wood (b. 1900), m. 22 October 1922 Cicely Aldous, 1 daughter Elizabeth Margaret Aldous (b. 1933)
7.3 Catherine Elizabeth Wood (b. 1902)
7.4 Joan Kathleen Wood (b. 1907)
7.5 Mary Patricia Wood (b. 1914)

APPENDIX 2

Sources

Manuscripts and Archives Research Library TCD

MS 4047–4218 Donation of Miss Doreen Boyle, 4 Shakespeare Street, Stratford-on-Avon, 11 August 1967, as heir of her cousin, Selina Boyle, Bushey Park, Enniskerry, Co. Wicklow

MS 4047–4170 Ina Boyle: Compositions (catalogued Síle Ní Thiarnaigh, Music Librarian)

MS 4171/1–11 Recordings (See Discography p. 161), I Boyle Memoranda Musical Compositions

MS 4173 Mrs Elizabeth LeFanu: Ina Boyle List of MS scores etc. of her compositions, 6 August 1967

MS 4174/1–19 Family photographs

MS 4175 66 Newspaper/Journal press cuttings 1918–1948

MS 4176–4218 Crampton Papers
(i) Photo: Selina A. P. Boyle (ii) Profiles and pathologist's report of body: Philip Crampton 17 May 1813, son of Sir Philip Crampton (iii) Photo: Mrs Boyle (iv) Two Sketches by Ina Boyle of Ann (Nancy) Crampton (1768–1857) sister of Sir Philip Crampton, wife of Lord Chief Justice Charles Kendall Bushe (1767–1843), Kilmurry House, Co. Kilkenny (from a pastel sketch property of her great-great-grandson, Sir Philip Coghill Bart)

MS 4184/5 Letter from Elizabeth Maconchy to Ina Boyle, 1934

MS 4058a Souvenir programme, Dublin Philharmonic Society concert, Theatre Royal Dublin, 16 March 1929

TCD MS 4172 I Boyle Memoranda Musical Compositions

digitalcollections.tcd.ie

88 items have been digitised from the 'Selina (Ina) Boyle Musical Manuscripts Miscellaneous' in TCD Manuscripts and Archives Research Library

Presented by the Bodleian Library Oxford, 19 June 1985
MS 10068 Letters from Mr Basil O'Connell genealogist, Adelaide Hutchins, Catherine Wood, Brigadier Maurice Jephson, Rev. Harry Darling (25 items)
MS 10069 Genealogical notes etc. on the Cramptons, Jephsons (22 folios)
MS 10070 Pencil sketches of Victoire Balfe copied by Ina Boyle from Print Room British Museum

Presented by Mr William LeFanu, 8 August 1994
MS 10715 Letters from Sheila Wingfield to Ina Boyle 1954–56 (10 items)

Presented by Professor Nicola LeFanu, 17 February 1997
MS 10959 A few notes on Lessons from Dr Vaughan Williams 1928–1939
MS 10959 Miscellaneous manuscripts and scores
MS 10960 Letter from C. H. Kitson, 19 March 1922

Presented by Professor Nicola LeFanu, 9 August 2007
MS 9308/674/1–4, 6, 7 Correspondence between Ina Boyle and Edith Sitwell, 12–25 February 1952
MS 9308/674/5 Letter from Máirín Allen, Hon. Sec., Art Section, Comhairle Oluimpeach na hÉireann, 15 February 1952

The Contemporary Music Centre
Vocal, choral, orchestral, instrumental scores

National Library of Ireland
(With the permission of the Board of the National Library of Ireland)
MS 29047 (4) Department of Manuscripts: Seven Letters from Ina Boyle to Sheila Wingfield (1938–1964)

Archive, Music Association of Ireland
PD 3094 TX Prints and Drawings: Sketches by Sir John Crampton and Selina Crampton

British Library
MS MUS–160 Letters from Ralph Vaughan Williams to Ina Boyle 1922–58 (By kind permission of Ursula Vaughan Williams)

National Archives Dublin
Last Will and Testaments:
20 October 1927: Philippa Arabella Boyle
23 February 1933: Phyllis Kathleen Boyle
15 February 1967: Selina Adelaide P. Boyle

St Patrick's Church of Ireland, Enniskerry
Parish Registers

National Archives of Scotland
GD 281/41/67 Ina Boyle and the Carnegie United Kingdom Trust (adjudication
 reports and correspondence)

Centre for Research Collections, Edinburgh University Library
Coll-44 Donald Francis Tovey to Ina Boyle, 17 September 1931

The Dominant ed. Edwin Evans, February 1928, 34 (OUP)
Review by Ina Boyle
Songs of the Irish Gaels eds Séamus Clandillon and Margaret Hannagan
This volume contains 75 songs collected and edited by Margaret Hannagan
and Séamus Clandillon and it includes four or five compositions by the editors.
Many of the tunes in the book have already been published in the collection
of Bunting, and the Feis Ceoil Irish Folksong Journal and others. Of 'The
Beggar' (20) and 'The Blackbird' (37) the editor says that he found the words in
a notebook of Bunting but there were no airs to them. But Bunting did publish
in one of his books two tunes of these names which would fit the words. 'The
Blackbird and the Thrush' has been arranged by Charles Wood with words by
Alfred Perceval Graves. The tune of 'Ned of the Hill' is not the traditional one
but is a version composed by Mrs Clandillon in 1901. She says in her note 'The
air is thoroughly Gaelic in structure and became at once immensely popular so
that it has passed into currency as the original "Eamonn an Cnuic"'. It is a pity
that the original tune was not given here as well, for a close imitation printed
among traditional airs might easily mislead someone who had not turned back
to the note. The last five songs in the book are settings of religious poems.
Some of the traditional religious poems which are common in both Ireland
and Scotland are extremely beautiful. There are runes and prayers, hymns and
blessings, as lovely as the best early English carols and fine translations of them
have been made by Dr A Carmichael, Miss Eleanor Hull, Professor Kuno
Meyer and others. In the present book the poems are fairly modern ... They are

not so simple and beautiful as the earlier religious poems, but they are the same type. The first given here, 'Hymn to the Sacred Heart', is set to a striking tune, 'In Fermoy one day', which is very like 'The Love-Wandering' in Mrs Kennedy Fraser's Songs of the Hill and is perhaps a variant of that tune.

The editors have added careful phrasing and breath marks to suit the Gaelic words and in the notes they give many details as to the collection of the songs. The collection will be especially useful in providing songs for music competition festivals where there are classes for singing in Irish as there are not many published songs with Gaelic words. It will probably also supply material for many arrangements as the songs are of varied types – drinking songs, love-songs, comic songs and working songs, and some are suitable for setting as part songs. The collection and singing of the airs has clearly been a labour of love and a lifelong interest of the editors. Their Foreword is this lovely verse from the Dialogue of Oisin and St Patrick.

> Melodious are thy lays, O Blackbird of Derrycarn!
> I have never heard in any place on earth
> Music sweeter than thy tune
> While perched beneath thy nest.

Catalogue of Compositions

A. WORKS WITH ORCHESTRA

Elegy (*Elegie*) for violoncello and orchestra (1913): vc-solo/2222/2100/timp/str
Piano score (17 January 1913) Title: *Romance*
Orchestral score (January 1913): Title changed to *Elegie*
First performance: 30 May 2016 Staatskapelle Weimar, conductor Paul Meyer,
cello Nadège Rochat

Old Ireland (1914): Bar-solo/satb/2222/4130/timp/str
Text: Walt Whitman

Soldiers at Peace (1916): satb/2222/4230/timp/hp/str
Carnegie Trust competition 1917: Commended and placed on a list of works of
special merit for the information of conductors
Text: Herbert Asquith
Published: Novello & Co. Ltd. (1917)
Dedicated 'To My Mother'
First performance: 6 February 1920, Woodbrook, Bray Choral Society, conductor
Thomas Weaving

Battle Hymn of the Republic (1918): S-solo/satb/2222/4230/ timp/hp/str
Text: Julia Ward Howe

Lo, in this day we keep our yesterdays (1919): Bar-solo/2222/ 4230/timp/str
Text: Francis Thompson

A Sea Poem (1918–19): 3(picc)3(corA)22/4231/perc/hp/str
Theme, six Variations, Finale

The Magic Harp (1919) Rhapsody for orchestra: 3(picc)3(corA)3(bcl)2/4231/timp/hp/str
Carnegie Trust competition 1920: Accepted for publication in Carnegie Collection of British Music. Patron's Fund: Accepted for performance
Published: Stainer & Bell (1921) for Carnegie United Kingdom Trust Publication Scheme
Dedicated 'To C. H. Kitson Mus.Doc.'
First performance: 8 July 1920, RCM, LSO, conductor Adrian Boult

Colin Clout (1921) Pastoral for orchestra. After the first Aeglogue of Spenser's *Shepheardes Calendar* revised (1923): 23(corA)3(bcl)2/4030/timp/hp/str
Patron's Fund: Accepted for performance
Dedicated 'To Phyllis'
First performance: 22 June 1922, RCM, (New) Queen's Hall Orchestra, conductor Adrian Boult

'Glencree' (in the Wicklow Hills) Symphony No. 1 (1924–27), 1st movement added 1927, revised 1928, 1937: 23(corA)3(bcl)2/4231/timp/hp/str; three movements: I 'On Lacken Hill' *Molto moderato*, II 'Night Winds in the Valley' *Allegro molto*, III 'Above Lough Bray' *Adagio*
Patron's Fund: Two movements accepted
First performance: One movement, *Adagio*, 4 December 1925, RCM, LSO, conductor Adrian Boult; 1st movement, *Molto moderato*, 26 January 1944, Radio Éireann 'Irish Music and Musicians', RÉO, conductor Arthur Duff; complete: 25 June 1945, Radio Éireann 'Irish Composers Ina Boyle', RÉO, conductor Arthur Duff

Hymne of heavenly love (1925–26 revised 1929): S-solo/ssaatb/23(corA) 22/4230/timp/hp/str
Text: Edmund Spenser

Phantasy for violin and chamber orchestra (1926) 11(cor A)11/2000/timp/hp/str

Psalm for violoncello and orchestra (1927 revised 1928): 23(corA)22/4230/timp/hp/str

The Dream of the Rood Symphony No. 2 (1929–30). After the Anglo-Saxon poem in the Vercelli Book tenth-century manuscript tr. Professor R. K. Gordon: 23(corA)3(bcl)2/4331/perc/hp/str; three movements: I *Adagio-Allegro*, II *Adagio*, III *Grave-Moderato, molto maestoso*

Virgilian Suite (1930–31) Ballet suite for small orchestra after the Eclogues of Virgil tr. T. F. Royde: 22(corA)11/2000/perc/hp/str; four movements: I Prelude, II Elegy, III Introduction and Fugue, IV Finale
First performance: II Elegy 30 November 1950, Metropolitan Hall, DOP, conductor Brian Boydell

Peace, peace! he is not dead (1932) Elegy for chorus and orchestra: satb/2222/4030/timp/str
Text: 'Adonais', Shelley

Concerto for violin and orchestra (1932–33 revised 1935): solo vl/2222/2130/timp/str/; three movements played without break: I *Lento ma non troppo*, II *Adagio*, III *Allegro ma non troppo*
Dedicated 'To the memory of my mother'
First performance: 26 April 1935, BBC London (rehearsed but not broadcast), BBC Orchestra, conductor Aylmer Buesst, violin André Mangeot
27 August 2010: Ulster Hall, Ulster Orchestra, conductor Kenneth Montgomery, violin Catherine Leonard (Recording: BBC Radio 3)

Overture for orchestra (1933–34): 2(picc)222/4231(btrb)/perc/hp/str
First performance: 27 February 1948, Phoenix Hall, RÉSO, conductor Jean Martinon

The Dance of Death (1935–36) Masque or ballet after the Woodcuts of Hans Holbein: 2(picc)222/4231/perc/str on stage tenor, voice and bagpipe
Text: translated from French by John Lydgate, speaking parts optional
The masque consists of a twelve-note theme (the hour-glass in Holbein)
Prelude, 17 Variations, Finale Masque: twenty-one chief characters plus twenty other parts
Copies of forty-nine original woodcuts inserted in score, twenty-two costume sketches
'All dresses are copied as closely as possible from Holbein. A complete set of the woodcuts is bound with the full score for reference, and watercolour reproductions of woodcuts, bound separately, are included ... These suggestions apply to the presentation of the work as a ballet, for television the Holbein designs should be followed as closely as possible.'

The Vision of Er (1938–39) A mimed Drama with Music founded on Book X of Plato's *The Republic*, translated A. D. Lindsay
Prelude, Scene I 'The Place of Judgement', Scene II 'The Choosing of the Lots', Scene III 'The Plain of Lethe': ssa(soli)/2222/4231/perc/hp/str
First performance: scene III, 4 October 1949, Phoenix Hall, RÉSO, conductor Brian Boydell

Hellas (1941) S-solo/satb/2222/4331/perc/hp/str 5 movements
Text: A Sequence of Epitaphs from The Greek Anthology, tr. J. W. Mackail
Dedicated 'To the memory of those who died for Greece'

Wildgeese (1942) Sketch for small orchestra: solo vc/2222/2000/timp/hp/str
Dedicated 'To Rev. Canon Henry Kingsmill Moore'
First performance: 26 January 1944, RÉO, conductor Arthur Duff, cello Clyde
Twelvetrees

The Prophet (1945): Bar-solo/2222/4230/perc/str
Text: Pushkin, translated Maurice Baring

From the Darkness Symphony No. 3 (1946–51) for contralto and orchestra:
C-solo/2 (picc)222/423[btrb]o/timp/hp/str; three movements: I 'Invocation',
Grave-Più Lento, II 'An Old Woman', *Andante tranquillo*, III 'Harvest', *Lento-
Allegro*
Text: Edith Sitwell

No coward soul is mine (1953): C-solo/str
Text: Emily Brontë
First performance: 28 April 1960, Wigmore Hall London, Kathleen Merrett
Orchestra, conductor Kathleen Merrett, contralto Janet Baker

B. CHORAL WORKS

Even such is time (1912): ssaattb and pf
Text: Walter Raleigh

O perfect love (1913) Anthem: S-solo/ssa/org
Dedicated to Sylvia May D'Olier Wix (1892–1998)

He will swallow up death in victory (1915) Funeral Anthem: S-solo/satb/org
Text: Isaiah XXV 8, 9
Published: Stainer & Bell (1915)
First performance: 16 March 1977, Monkstown Parish Church, Radio Éireann
Singers, conductor Michael Bowles

Wilt not Thou, O God, go forth with our hosts? (1915) Anthem for Intercession:
satb/org
Text: from Psalms 108, 33
Dedicated 'To the 36ᵗʰ (Ulster) Division'
Published: Novello & Co. Ltd. (1915)
First performance: 18 September 2014, St Columb's Cathedral, Derry

The Transfiguration (1921) Anthem: T-solo/satb/org
Text: Selected by Canon Kingsmill Moore
Published: Novello & Co. (1923)
Dedicated 'To the Rev. Canon Kingsmill Moore DD, Canon of St. Patrick's'
First performance: 26 November 1922, St Patrick's Cathedral, conductor Dr
George Hewson

Gaelic Hymns (1923–24, 1929): unaccompanied chorus sixteen hymns
Text: *Carmina Gadelica* Gaelic hymns and invocations collected in the Hebrides
and Western Highlands of Scotland, translated Alexander Carmichael
Published: nos. 1–5 (1923) J. & W. Chester (1930)
Dedicated 'For Mother'
1. Jesu, Thou Son of Mary' ssattb, 2. 'The guardian angel' ttbb C-solo, 3. 'The
light'ner of the stars' ssattb, 4. 'The soul leading' satb C-solo, 5. 'Soul peace'
satb
First performance: *Four Gaelic Hymns*, 10 March 1931, Aeolian Hall London,
Oriana Madrigal Society, conductor Charles Kennedy Scott, alto soloist Mary
Morris
Unpublished hymns:
     1923: 'God be with me lying down' ssattb C-solo, 'Jesu who ought to be
     praised' satb
     1924: 'Morning prayer' ssatb, 'O Jesu! Tonight' ssatb, 'God be with us'
     ssattb, Bar-solo satb, 'A sleep prayer' ssaa, 'A prayer for grace' ttbb, bass-
     solo, 'Christmas Carol' satb
     1929: 'Lift Thou my soul to Thee' satb, 'A Blessing' satb [first setting], A
     Blessing' ssattb [second setting]

Caedmon's Hymn (1925): ssattb
Text: translated from Anglo-Saxon L. Magnus and C. Headlam

Service and Strength, Hymn for St Michael and All Saints, 'Enniskerry' (1929):
satb
Text: Christina Rossetti
Published: *Songs of Praise* OUP (1930)

Leave me, O love (1930–33): satb
Text: Sir Philip Sidney

If God build not the house (1930–33): satb
Text: Psalm CXXVII Phineas Fletcher

He that hath eternal being (1930–33): satb
Text: Psalms of David no. 48 (Sir Philip Sidney and the Countess of Pembroke)
'As high as highest Heav'n', 'The shining Lord He is my light', 'O lovely thing',
'Lord before Thee I do lay', 'Be still, saith He', 'O laud the Lord'

Holy art Thou (1931): ssattb
Text: Cynewulf's Christ, tr. R. K. Gordon

Jesu, that dear boughtest me (1931): satb
Text: fourteenth-century poem Vernon manuscripts, Early English Texts Society

A Spanish Pastoral (1931): S-solo or boys' voices in unison/ttb
Text: St Teresa, tr. Arthur Symons
Published: Stainer & Bell (1935)
First performance: Recording for documentary *From the Darkness*, RTÉ Lyric
FM, 5 June 2010, Honan Chapel Chamber Choir, director Sonya Keogh

Good Friday (1934): satb
Text: Abelard, tr. Helen Waddell

Hunger and thirst, O Christ (1934) Motet: satb
Text: Radbod, Bishop of Utrecht, tr. Helen Waddell

Seven Psalms (1936): ssatb/S-solo/Bar-solo ad lib
Text: Psalms of David 57, 27, 92, 38, 46, 23, 150
(Philip Sidney and the Countess of Pembroke)

Love is the plant of peace (1937): satb
Text: William Langland

O Thou! Whose Spirit (1940) Motet: satb
Text: Henry Vaughan
First performance: October 2000, autumn tour, National Chamber Choir,
conductor Colin Mawby

Blessed be the Lord, for He hath showed me His marvellous kindness (1952–54)
Cantata: Mez-solo/satb/org

The spacious firmament on high (1954) Motet: ssaatb
Text: Joseph Addison
First performance: 5 October 2013, Evensong St Paul's Cathedral, London

Ye flaming powers (1961) Motet: Bar-solo/ssa
Text: John Milton

C. CHAMBER WORKS

Phantasy for viola and pianoforte (1918)
First performance: 12 February 2015, CIT Cork School of Music, David Kenny
viola, Ciara Moroney piano

Christ is a path (1925) Chamber cantata: S-solo/fl/ob/cor angl(or cl)/str quar
Three versions: six songs with instrumental interludes
1. 'Christ is a path', 2. 'Who can forget never to be forgot', 3. 'When I remember
Christ', 4. 'Drop, drop slow tears', 5. 'It was but now their sounding clamours
sung', 6. 'See where the author of all life'
Text: Giles and Phineas Fletcher
First performance: 1, 2, 4: 27 June 1933, BBC Cardiff, Beatrice Pugh soprano

A dream in May morning (1927): S-solo/str quar
Text: Geoffrey Chaucer

String Quartet in E minor (1934, revised 1934, 1935, 1937); three movements:
I. *Allegro moderato*, II. *Adagio*, III. *Allegro molto*
Dedicated 'To Anne Macnaghten'
First performance: 15 July 1937, BBC London, Macnaghten Quartet

Thinke then, my soule (1938): T-solo/str quar
Text: John Donne from the 'Second Anniversarie'
Published: OUP (1939)
First performance: 16 December 1942, BBC London, Zorian String Quartet,
Harold Bradbury tenor

Faith (1941) Elegy: T-solo/fl/hp/str quar
Text: Anon, *The Daily Telegraph*, 16 Jan. 1941
'The elder of two brothers, both flight lieutenants, was killed on active service
on Christmas Eve. The younger wrote home saying that while thinking of his
brother as he invariably did in the evenings words suddenly framed themselves
in his mind. He felt he must write them down which he did at once with
scarcely a pause for thought.'

Urania (1942): Mez-solo/str quar
Text: Ruth Pitter

Lament for Bion (1944–45): T-solo/str quar or orch
Text: Moschus tr. J. M. Edmonds
Awarded commemoration medal and Diplome d'Honneur in music category
Olympic Art Competition, London, 1948

Hymne To God my God, in my sicknesse (1946): T-solo/str quar
Text: John Donne
Dedicated 'Intended for 86th birthday of my father [5 September 1946] but
not finished'
First performance: 13 October 1947, Radio Éireann, 'Music by Contemporary
Irish Composers', Cuala Quartet, Robert McCullagh tenor

Still falls the rain (1948): C-solo/str quar
Text: Edith Sitwell
First performance: 1964, Saffron Walden, Macnaghten Quartet (Anne
Macnaghten, Bernard Blay, Pauline Jackson, Arnold Ashby), Margaret Cable
mez sop

Three songs by Ben Jonson (1955) 1. 'It was a beauty that I saw', 2. 'Witch's charm',
3. 'Flow, flow, fresh fount': medium voice/vl/vc
Text: Ben Jonson
Dedicated 'For Anne and Arnold Ashby'
First performance: 1964, Saffron Walden, Anne Macnaghten, Arnold Ashby,
Margaret Cable mez sop

Three ancient Irish poems (1958) 1. 'Eve's lament', 2. 'Lament for youth', 3. 'Winter
song': S-solo/vla/hp
Text: tr. Kuno Meyer
First performance: 21 May 2017, Monkstown Parish Church, Lynda Lee
soprano, Lisa Dowdall viola, Andreja Malir harp

D. OPERA

Maudlin of Paplewick (1956?–1964)
A Chamber Opera in Three Acts [The prose synopsis of the libretto with which
the composer prefaces the full score divides the opera into a Prologue and three
Acts. The full score itself, however, has no separate Prologue and the relevant
text is instead incorporated into the beginning of Act 1]
Libretto based on *The Sad Shepherd, or A Tale of Robin Hood*, an unfinished
pastoral play by Ben Jonson

Cast: Eighteen singing roles, two young woodmen (dancers), three musicians (onstage miming), foresters etc.
Orchestra: fl/ob/bsn/hn/timp/hp/str.quintet [2vln, vla, vc, db]

E. VOCAL MUSIC

'Snow-flakes' (Henry Wadsworth Longfellow), 'The winds as at their hour of birth' (Tennyson), 'Cradle song' (St John Lucas), 'A song of a nest' (Jean Ingelow) (1903)

'The cry' (L. G. Moberly), 'Sea Wrack' (Moira O'Neill) (1905)

'Scythe song' (Andrew Lang) (1906)

'Do you remember still?' (L. G. Moberly), 'A cradle song' (T.J.H.), 'The high tide' (Joan Ingelow) (1907)

'Not yet' (L. G. Moberly) (1908)

'The lost water', 'Roses', 'The well at the world's end' (Eva Gore-Booth), 'The wind of dreams', 'Life's harvest' (R. M. Marriott Watson) (1909)

'Hungarian song' (M. Byron), 'In prison' (William Morris), 'A soft day, thank God' (Winifred M. Letts), 'Potter's song' (Longfellow) (1912)

'Midwinter' (Kujohara No Fukayabu, tr. Clara Walsh), 'The last invocation' (Walt Whitman) (1913)

'Lullaby' (Maurice Hime), 'The joy of earth' (George Russell (Æ)) (1914)
First performance: 5 May 1915, Arcadia Barracks Bray, Nora Borel soprano, Rev. Arthur Oulton piano

'Have you news of my boy Jack?' (Rudyard Kipling) (1916)
First performance: 9 November 2015, Fr McNally Recital Room, Dundalk Institute of Technology, Páidí Ó Dubháin baritone

'A song of enchantment', 'A song of shadows' (Walter de la Mare) (1922)
Published: Stainer & Bell (1923, 1926)
Dedicated 'To my Mother'
First performance: 13 October 1947, Radio Éireann, Jean Nolan mez sop, Rhoda Coghill piano

'If you let sorrow in on you' (W. M. Letts) (1922)
Dedicated to Sylvia Duckworth
First performance: 23 August 2013, Kilruddery House, Regina Nathan soprano, Anne Cullen piano

'Cum invocarum' (Philip Sidney) (1923)

'Sleep song' ['Deirín Dé'] (1923) (tr. from the traditional Irish by P. H. Pearse, published *The Irish Review*, May 1911, 139ff.)
First performed: Radio Éireann, 13 October 1947, Jean Nolan mez sop, Rhoda Coghill piano

Two Christmas Songs 1. 'So blyssid be the tyme' (Sloane MS), 2. 'Tyrle tyrlow' (Balliol MS) (1923)
Dedicated 'For Mother. Christmas 1923'

'Eternity' (Robert Herrick) (1924)
Dedicated 'In memory of Rev. H.S. Mecredy' [incumbent Powerscourt 1907–24], d. 14 December 1924
First performance: 13 October 1947, Radio Éireann, Jean Nolan mez sop, Rhoda Coghill piano

'Since thou O fondest and truest', 'Spring goeth all in white' (Robert Bridges) (1924)

'Longing' (George Herbert) (1925), 'The bringer of dreams' (Edith Sitwell) (1925, revised 1927)

'The stolen child' (W. B. Yeats), 'Blow, blow, thou winter wind' (Shakespeare), 'They went forth' (Eva Gore-Booth) (1926)

'When Mary thro' the garden went' (Mary Coleridge) (1927)
Dedicated 'For Mother's birthday'
First performance: 5 June 2010, Documentary *From the Darkness*, RTÉ Lyric FM, Sonya Keogh, mez sop, David Brophy piano

'A mountain woman asks for quiet that her child may sleep' (P. H. Pearse, tr. T. MacDonagh), 'Blessing' (Austin Clarke) (1928)
First performance: 23 August 2013, Kilruddery House, Regina Nathan soprano, Anne Cullen piano

'The Land: Prelude, Winter, Spring' (Vita Sackville-West) (1928)

'All Souls' Flower' (Pamela Grey of Falloden), A Christmas carol (1928)
Dedicated 'Written for my mother at Christmas, the last of her Christmas or birthday songs ... I used the tune of this in the third movement of my violin concerto, dedicated to the memory of my mother.'
First performance: 5 June 2010, Documentary *From the Darkness*, RTÉ Lyric FM, Sonya Keogh mez sop, David Brophy piano

'Himself and his fiddle' (E. L. Twiss) (1929)

Five Sacred Folksongs of Sicily (translated Grace Warrack) 1. 'Eternal love', 2. 'In the desert', 3. 'The yoke', 4. 'Lord in that love', 5. 'At the altar' (1930)

'Dust' Epigram (1933)

'Praier of Pieus Mirandula unto God' (Thomas More) (1937)

'Easter snow' (W. M. Letts) (1940)
Dedicated 'In memory of S. who died 12 Nov. 1939'

'With sick and famished eyes' Song by Henry Purcell (George Herbert) ed. Ina Boyle for voice with piano (or harpsichord) and violoncello ad lib.
Published: OUP (1943)

Three Mediaeval Latin Lyrics (1953) 1. 'Sleep', 2. 'Storm', 3. 'Evening on the Moselle' (translated Helen Waddell) (1953)
Dedicated 'Written for Sophie Wyss'
First performance: 4 April 1955, Drawing Room Arts Council, Joan Gray mez sop, Eric Stevens piano

Two Songs of the Woods (1954) 1. 'Dirge in the woods', 2. 'Enter these enchanted woods' (George Meredith)
First performance: 4 April 1955, Drawing Room Arts Council, Joan Gray mez sop, Eric Stevens piano

Three Songs by Walter de la Mare (1956) 1. 'Song of the mad prince', 2. 'The pigs and the charcoal-burner', 3. 'Moon, reeds, rushes'
Dedicated 'For Ina Jephson'
First performance: 2 January 1968, Radio Éireann, Patricia McCarry sop, Rhoda Coghill piano

Looking Back (1961–66) 1. 'Carrowdore' (St John Ervine), 2. 'All Souls' night' (Frances Cornford), 3. 'O ghost that has gone' (James Stephens), 4. 'The Mill Water' (Edward Thomas)

First performance: 'O ghost that has gone', 5 June 2010, Documentary *From the Darkness*, RTÉ Lyric FM, Sonya Keogh mez sop, David Brophy piano

APPENDIX 4

Performances during Ina Boyle's Lifetime: 1915–67

Title	Date	Venue
'The joy of earth'	5 May 1915	Arcadia Barracks, Bray, Nora Borel sop., Arthur Oulton piano
Soldiers at Peace	6 February 1920	Woodbrook, Bray Choral Society, cond. Thomas Weaving
The Magic Harp	8 July 1920	RCM, LSO, cond. Adrian Boult
	16 December 1921	Bournemouth, Bournemouth Symphony Orchestra, cond. Dan Godfrey
	6 September 1923	Promenade Concert, Queen's Hall, (New) Queen's Hall Orchestra, cond. Sir Henry Wood
	13 January 1927	Bournemouth, Bournemouth Symphony Orchestra, cond. Sir Dan Godfrey
	28 November 1927	Queen's Hall, National Symphony Orchestra, cond. Sir Landon Ronald
	16 March 1929	Theatre Royal Dublin, Dublin Philharmonic Society, cond. Fritz Brase
	4 November 1929	RDS, Dublin Philharmonic Society, cond. Fritz Brase
	26 January 1944	Radio Éireann, RÉO, cond. Arthur Duff
	25 June 1945	Radio Éireann, RÉO, cond. Arthur Duff
	1949	Palma de Mallorca, Orquesta Sinfónica de Mallorca, cond. Ahn Eak Tai
	28 June 1955	Abbey Lecture Hall, RÉO, cond. Éimear Ó Broin

Title	Date	Venue
Colin Clout	22 June 1922	RCM, LSO, cond. Adrian Boult
	1 April 1936	Aula Maxima, University College Cork, CSO, cond. Aloys Fleischmann
	24 April 1938	Gaiety Theatre, RÉO, cond. Aloys Fleischmann
	26 January 1944	Radio Éireann, RÉO, cond. Arthur Duff
	21 November 1949	Palma de Mallorca, Orquesta Sinfónica de Mallorca, cond. Ahn Eak Tai
The Transfiguration	26 November 1922	St Patrick's Cathedral, Cathedral Choir
Symphony No. 1 'Glencree'	4 December 1925	RCM, one movement, *Adagio*, LSO, cond. Adrian Boult
	26 January 1944	Radio Éireann, 1st movement, *Molto moderato*, RÉSO, cond. Arthur Duff
	25 June 1945	Radio Éireann, RÉO, cond. Arthur Duff
Gaelic Hymns	10 March 1931	Aeolian Hall, Oriana Madrigal Society, cond. Charles Kennedy Scott
	30 May 1933	Aeolian Hall, Oriana Madrigal Society, cond. Charles Kennedy Scott
	1 August 1947	Dept. of Ed. Summer School Choir, cond. Charles Kennedy Scott
	27 January 1948	Waterford Music Club, Tramore Singers, cond. Stella Jacob
	29 June 1948	Wigmore Hall, Oriana Madrigal Society, cond. Charles Kennedy Scott
	19 November 1956	Arts Council London, Purcell Singers, cond. Imogen Holst
	28 April 1964	Radio Éireann, RTÉ Singers, cond. Hans Waldemar Rosen
Violin Concerto	26 April 1935	Rehearsal BBC Symphony Orchestra, cond. Aylmer Buesst, violin Andre Mangeot
Christ is a path	27 June 1935	BBC Cardiff, movements 1, 2, 4, Beatrice Pugh sop.
String Quartet in E minor	15 July 1937	BBC London, Macnaghten String Quartet

Title	Date	Venue
Thinke then, my soule	16 December 1942	BBC London, Harold Bradbury ten., Zorian Quartet
	5 May 1945	Broadcast Beverley Minster, René Soames ten., Hirsch Quartet
	13 October 1947	Radio Éireann, Robert McCullagh ten., Cuala Quartet
	1952	Oxford, Ladies Musical Society, David Galliver ten.
	4 November 1965	Radio Éireann, Patrick Ring ten., David Lillis, Janos Furst, Máire Larchet, Maurice Meulien
Wildgeese	22 January 1944	Radio Éireann, RÉO, cond. Arthur Duff
	25 January 1945	Radio Éireann, RÉO, cond. Arthur Duff
	18 November 1947	Phoenix Hall, RÉSO, cond. Edmond Appia
	25 January 1948	Capitol Theatre, RÉSO, cond. Edmond Appia
	14 June 1949	Phoenix Hall, RÉO, cond. Arthur Duff
	9 January 1955	Gaiety Theatre, RÉSO, cond. Milan Horvat
Overture for orchestra	27 February 1948	Phoenix Hall, RÉSO, cond. Jean Martinon
'A song of enchantment', 'A song of shadows', 'Sleep song', 'Eternity'	13 October 1947	Radio Éireann, Jean Nolan mez. sop., Rhoda Coghill piano
'A song of enchantment'	29 April 1954	Radio Éireann, Patricia Thomas sop., Rhoda Coghill piano
Hymne To God, my God, in my sicknesse	13 October 1947	Radio Éireann, Robert McCullagh ten., Cuala Quartet
The Vision of Er, Scene III	4 October 1949	Phoenix Hall, RÉSO, cond. Brian Boydell
Virgilian Suite, II Elegy	30 November 1950	Metropolitan Hall, DOP cond. Brian Boydell

Title	Date	Venue
Three Mediaeval Latin Lyrics, Two Songs of the Woods	4 April 1955	Arts Council, London, Joan Gray mez. sop., Eric Stephens piano
No coward soul is mine	28 April 1960	Wigmore Hall, Kathleen Merrett Orchestra, Janet Baker mez. sop.
Still falls the rain, Three Songs by Ben Jonson	1964	Saffron Walden, Macnaghten String Quartet, Margaret Cable mez. sop.

Notes and References

PREFACE

1   Elizabeth Maconchy, *Ina Boyle: An Appreciation, with a Select List of her Music* (Dublin: Dolmen Press, 1974), p. 3.

1. THE GROWTH OF A COMPOSER

1   *Irish Times*, 11 March 1889.

2   A bust of Sir Philip Crampton by Christopher Moore is displayed in the entrance hall of the RCSI. His town house, 14 Merrion Square, Dublin, where a pear tree grew in the basement, is mentioned by James Joyce in *Finnegans Wake*. The Crampton Memorial (1862) by Joseph Kirk, a bust with three swans above drinking fountains surmounted by a cascade of metal foliage, stood at the junction of College Street and Great Brunswick Street (now Pearse Street). It was removed due to its poor condition and not replaced. It is mentioned twice in *Ulysses* (Chapters 6 and 8) and in *A Portrait of the Artist as a Young Man*: 'Is the bust of Sir Philip Crampton lyrical, epical or dramatic?' (Oxford: OUP, 2000), p. 180.

3   Crampton papers, TCD MS 4176–4218.

4   See Basil Walsh, *Michael W. Balfe* (Dublin: Irish Academic Press, 2008), pp. 157ff.

5   The list of paintings bequeathed by Ina Boyle to the Ashmolean Museum included watercolours by David Cox, Samuel Prout and Thomas Rowlandson and oil paintings by John Morland, Guardi, David Tenniers, as well as engravings by Watteau.

6   A total of eighty-four sketches by Sir John Crampton and Selina Crampton are preserved in the Prints and Drawings Collection of the NLI (PD 3094 TX).

7   Her cousin, William Crampton Gore RHA (b. Enniskerry 1871, d. 1946), friend of Orpen and Augustus John, was a well-known artist.

8   In 1911 he entered three violins for the RDS Art Industries Exhibition which were commended, highly commended and awarded first prize of one guinea.

9   In her will Boyle left her violoncello (John Betts), viola (George Foster) and two violins (R. Duke and Klotz) to the Royal College of Music, 'to be given in the absolute discretion of the Principal ... to Students who may be unable to afford suitable instruments'.

10   Samuel Spencer Myerscough, b. Salford, FRCO (1873), Mus.Bac.Oxon, Hertford College (1881).

11   A copy of Myerscough's prize-winning motet, inscribed 'Kind regards S.S.M.', was preserved by Ina with her manuscripts.

12   *Musical Herald*, 1 July 1909.

13   All Myerscough quotations are from TCD MS 4051.

14   Eva Gore-Booth, *Unseen Kings* (London: Longmans, Green, 1904), pp. 63ff. The poem was published in *Longman's Magazine* in 1903.

15   Adelaide Elizabeth Wills-Sandford, née Jephson (1850–1880), m Captain William Robert Wills-Sandford (1844–1889), Captain 2nd Dragoons and Royal Scots Greys, 26 March 1874.

Children: Charlotte (1875–1940), Mary Adelaide (1877–1956), Thomas George (1879–1956). She is buried in St Patrick's Churchyard, Powerscourt, Co. Wicklow.

16 *Music & Letters*, vii, no. 4, p. 393.

17 All Wood quotations are from TCD MS 4049.

18 Wood was attending the Leeds Festival for the first performance on 7 October 1904 of his new work for baritone, chorus and orchestra, *The Ballad of Dundee* (*Musical Times*, xlv, 741, p. 731).

19 Dr Percy Buck (1871–1947), BA, BMus, MA, DMus (Oxford).

20 TCD MS 4047.

21 *Musical Times*, lxxxv, 1216, p. 191.

22 TCD MS 4050.

23 TCD MS 4172.

24 John Coates (1865–1941), English tenor, sang with the principal opera companies, and gave a concert in Woodbrook, Bray, in January 1914.

25 Sir Herbert Hamilton Harty (1879–1941), organist, Christ Church, Bray, from 1896 to 1901, when he moved to London.

26 Sir Stanley Cochrane (1877–1949), athlete, music patron, mineral water manufacturer.

27 Victor Love (1890–1946), pupil of Esposito, later performed in London with the LPO and the LSO.

28 *Freeman's Journal*, 11–16 August 1913.

29 *Irish Times*, 5 February 1914.

30 *Irish Times*, 6 February 1914.

31 *Irish Times*, 21 February; 3, 4, 5, 6, 7, 8 August 1914.

32 *Irish Times*, 6 May 1915.

33 Kipling's son John was killed in the battle of Loos in October 1915. The most famous setting of the song, by Edward German, was recorded by Clara Butt in 1917 and also by Louise Kirkby Lunn.

34 *Irish Times*, 24 April 1919.

35 'Memoranda', p. 3: 'This was to have been sung by the choir of Derry Cathedral but so many of the men went to the war that it could not be given.' On 18 September 2016 the anthem was sung in St Columb's Cathedral on the occasion of the dedication of a commemorative cross in memory of those who died in the battle of the Somme.

36 'Memoranda'. She also sent a copy to Charles Wood, 'who said he liked it'.

37 *Musical Times*, lix, 900, p. 69.

38 *The Times*, 23 February 1918.

39 Thomas Henry Weaving (1881–1966), professor RIAM, organist Christ Church Cathedral 1920–50.

40 'Memoranda', p. 4: 'Later Mrs T. Griffiths of Belfast saw the score and rehearsed it but owing to the troubled state of Belfast the concert fell through, but it was given with piano accompaniment.'

41 *Irish Times*, 7 February 1920.

42 Cobbett competition winners included Frank Bridge, John Ireland and Benjamin Britten.

43 'Memoranda', p. 4.

44 'Memoranda', p. 6. MS 4057a, Charles Wood corrected it and suggested revisions.

45 Ibid.

46 Ibid.

47 *Daily Mail*, 22 May 1920.

48 'Memoranda', p. 6.

49 *Morning Post*, 9 July 1920.

50 *Pall Mall Gazette*, 10 July 1920.
51 *Daily Telegraph*, 9 July 1920.
52 *Sunday Evening Telegraph*, 11 July 1920.
53 *The Strad*, August 1920.
54 *Musical Times*, lxii, 936, p. 123.
55 'Memoranda', p. 6.
56 *Daily Telegraph*, 15 July 1922.
57 *Musical Opinion*, August 1922.
58 *Musical Times*, lxiii, 955, p. 642.
59 *Musical News & Herald*, 19 August 1922.
60 *Evening Standard*, 22 May 1920.
61 *Morning Post*, 7 September 1923.
62 *The Times*, 29 November 1927. Broadcast BBC 2LO London and 5XX Daventry.
63 *Daily Telegraph*, 29 November 1927.
64 *Sunday Times*, 4 December 1927.
65 C. H. Kitson to Ina Boyle, 22 March 1922 from 60 Queensboro' Tce., Hyde Park.
66 Ibid.
67 *Irish Times*, 24 November 1922.
68 *Irish Times*, 27 November 1922.

2. LESSONS IN LONDON

1   Telephone conversation with Mrs Joan Stokes, Enniskerry, Co. Wicklow.
2   The first envelope is postmarked 22 December 1922.
3   B. L. Unincorporated MS Deposit 1997/05. Added pencil note [in Elizabeth Maconchy's hand] 'not found 1967' with arrow pointing to note re Ursula Vaughan Williams' letter.
4   TCD MS 10959. Unless otherwise noted all quotations relating to lessons with Vaughan Williams are from this source.
5   *Musical News & Herald*, June 1922.
6   *The Strad*, July 1922.
7   *Morning Post*, 22 June 1922.
8   *The Times*, 23 June 1922.
9   'Memoranda', p. 7.
10 Ibid. The original score with Vaughan Williams' notes and corrections revised September 1923, TCD MS 4171.
11 'Memoranda', p. 12.
12 Vaughan Williams himself had taken lessons in orchestration from Gordon Jacob.
13 See Appendix 2.
14 19 November 1927, pp. 88–93. Dr Donal O'Sullivan (1893–1973), Clerk of the Irish Senate, editor *Journal of the Irish Folk Song Society* (1927–39).
15 26 November, 3 December 1927.
16 The International Society for Contemporary Music (founded 1923) held annual festivals and competitions.
17 'Memoranda', p. 13.
18 'He said "I am rather a heretic about E.S." meaning I think that he thought her over-rated.'
19 She entered it for the ISCM festival in 1928 but it was not accepted.
20 'Sent it by Dr V.W.'s advice to Joan Elwes who said she would sing it if she had a suitable opportunity. She afterwards returned it saying she had none': 'Memoranda', p. 18.
21 Colonel Wilhelm Fritz Brase (1875–1940), graduate of the Leipzig Hochschule für Musik, came to Dublin in 1923 to establish the Army School of Music.

22 Centre for Research Collections, Edinburgh University Library: Tovey to Boyle. Coll. 411. 17 September 1931. On 24 December 1941 Boyle wrote to Hubert Foss, enclosing Tovey's letter.

23 Elizabeth Maconchy's symphonic suite, 'The Land' (1929), was premiered at the Proms in 1930.

24 8 April 1930, BL MS MUS-160.

25 In July 1931 while she was at the Festival, Ina Boyle had her photograph taken by A. G. Saywell, Arcade Studio, Oxford.

26 *Musical Times*, lxxi, 1053, p. 989.

27 *Musical Opinion*, July 1931.

28 Envelope postmarked 22 March 1931.

29 *The Times*, 11 March 1931.

30 *Musical Times*, lxxiv, 1085, p. 642.

31 The third movement of the concerto was based on a Christmas carol, 'All Souls Flower', composed for her mother (1928).

32 At the interview Evans said that he had recommended the work several times for performance. When the Camargo Society amalgamated with the Vic-Wells Ballet Company he returned the score and suggested that Boyle write to Constant Lambert, which she did, but it was not performed.

33 Boyle also entered it for the ISCM competition. It was rejected by both.

34 In her will Boyle left the surgeon, who was a literary scholar, a bequest of 'any books from my library which he may select ... in grateful remembrance of his kindness to me when ill'.

35 Her sister, Phyllis, was having treatment for a heart condition.

36 Adeline Vaughan Williams to Ina Boyle, 4 April 1934.

37 *Musical Times*, lxxvi, 1114, p. 1092.

38 Ralph Vaughan Williams to Ina Boyle, 4 May 1937.

39 1922, 1924 and 1925 (when Harty received an Honorary Doctorate from TCD).

40 Richard Pine, *Music and Broadcasting in Ireland* (Dublin: Four Courts Press, 2005), pp. 35ff.

41 Harold R. White (Dermot Macmurrough) (1872–1943), singer, organist, music critic, composer of 'Macushla'.

42 *Irish Times*, 18 March 1929, signed 'Obbligato'.

43 *Irish Independent*, 18 March 1929, signed 'Fugato'.

44 *Daily Mail*, 18 March 1929.

45 H.F.N[orman], *The Irish Statesman*, 23 March 1929.

46 *Irish Independent*, 5 November 1929. The evening programme included White's 'Autolycus' overture.

47 Séamas de Barra, *Aloys Fleischmann* (Dublin: Field Day Publications, 2006), p. 41.

48 *Cork Examiner*, 11 April 1936.

49 *Evening Echo*, 2 April 1936.

50 *Irish Independent*, 24 April 1938.

51 *Irish Times*, 24 April 1938.

52 Kitty Clive, 'Echoes of the Town', *Irish Times*, 14 April 1938.

53 The first performance of the 9th symphony was given by the RPO, conductor Sir Malcolm Sargent, at the Royal Festival Hall, 2 April 1958.

54 Viscountess Sheila Powerscourt, *née* Beddington, poet and memoirist (1906–1992), m. Meryvn Patrick Wingfield, 1932.

55 Ina Boyle to Sheila Wingfield, 14 December 1958.

3. A Changing World

1   Quoted by Michael Dawney, *Irish Times*, 23 March 1977.

2   Elizabeth Maconchy to Ina Boyle, 7 June 1934. In 1940 Ina Boyle orchestrated Maconchy's ballet, *Puck Fair*, for its first performance in the Gaiety Theatre Dublin.

3   Anne Macnaghten, 'The Story of the Macnaghten Concerts', *Musical Times*, c 1399, 460.

4   The recording is located in MS Library TCD: 4171/1–4.

5   Ina Boyle to Sheila Wingfield, 26 November 1938.

6   *Irish Times*, 23 July 1938.

7   Ibid., 30 April 1945.

8   Selina Jephson, psychic, pioneer of ESP, d. London, 15 October 1961.

9   Adelaide Hutchins, Thorneywood House, Bransgore, Christchurch, Hants, whose first husband, Captain Grenville Fortescue, was killed in action in 1915. She married Lt. Col. Francis Hutchins in 1930.

10 Sir Dermot Alexander Boyle GCB, KCVO, KBE, AFC (1904–1993), first graduate of the RAF College, Cranwell, to be appointed Chief of Air Staff (1956).

11 Her efforts to promote the work continued. She sent the score to David Willcocks at King's College, Cambridge, in 1959 and to Melville Cook, Hereford Cathedral, for consideration for the Three Choirs Festival in 1961.

12 'Gave it to Doreen Boyle to try. She played it to J[ohan] Hock, [conductor of the Birmingham Philharmonic String Orchestra] and intends to try it with others', 'Memoranda', p. 12.

13 Michael Bowles (1909–1998), Acting Director of Music RÉ, 1941; Director of Music, 1944; resigned January 1948.

14 At a meeting of WAAMA (forerunner of Actors' Equity) held in the Gate Theatre in 1944, Michael O'Higgins claimed that musicians engaged to augment the permanent orchestra were only paid two shillings per hour – one shilling for a Beethoven symphony. *Dublin Evening Post*, 31 January 1944.

15 The Department of Finance stipulated that the total charge on public funds was not to exceed £90 per concert. Michael Bowles, 'The Birth of the RÉSO', *Irish Times*, 6 February 1973.

16 Dr Arthur Duff (1899–1956), Acting Director of Music RÉ, 1942; Assistant Music Director, 1945.

17 Broadcast Radio Éireann, 26 January 1944.

18 Broadcast Radio Éireann, 25 June 1945. 'Lent full score to Mr W. Watson with a view to making an organ arrangement of 1st movement.' He returned the score on 13 April 1946 ('Memoranda', p. 14). William J. Watson, organist Christ Church Cathedral (1947–55), studied composition with Ina Boyle.

19 *Musical Times*, lxxxv, 1213, p. 87.

20 Awards for arts categories were given as part of the Olympic Games from 1912 to 1948 and again in 1952.

4. Post War

1   Superintendent Charles O'Donnell Sweeney, Director of Music, Garda Síochána, 1941–1950.

2   Broadcast Radio Éireann, 13 October 1947.

3   Others who attended in 1948 included composers Brian Boydell, Brendan Dunne, Joseph Groocock, Thomas Kelly, Edgar Deale, Walter Beckett, Havelock Nelson and conductor Éimear Ó Broin.

4   Broadcast Radio Éireann, 1 August 1947.

5 *Radio Review*, 18 November 1947, 25 January 1948.
6 *Radio Review*, 23 January 1948.
7 Among her press cuttings Boyle kept two undated reviews from Spanish newspapers of a concert at which *The Magic Harp* was conducted by Ahn Eak Tai.
8 *Irish Times*, 15 June 1949.
9 *Radio Review*, 30 September 1949. The work had been rejected by both the ISCM Committee and the Edinburgh Festival competition.
10 *Radio Review*, 24 November 1950.
11 *Irish Independent*, 5 October 1949.
12 Ina Boyle to Edith Sitwell, 12 February 1952.
13 Edith Sitwell to Ina Boyle, 25 February 1952.
14 Sheila Wingfield to Ina Boyle, 2 May 1955.
15 Ina Boyle to MAI, 22 March 1948.
16 Ibid.
17 MAI Papers, Manuscript Library, NLI, Box 7.
18 In 1976 the Composers' Group merged with the Association of Young Irish Composers to form the Association of Irish Composers.
19 Axel Klein, 'Brian Boydell: Of man and music', *The Life and Music of Brian Boydell* (Dublin: Irish Academic Press, 2004), p. 9.
20 Edgar Deale (ed.), *A Catalogue of Contemporary Irish Composers* (Dublin: MAI, 1968).
21 Ibid. (2nd ed. Dublin: MAI, 1973).
22 Elizabeth Maconchy notes in her handwritten catalogue that Dr Rosen had twelve copies of the motet, so it may have been performed by the Radio Éireann Singers.
23 *Musical Times*, lxxxxvi, 1348, p. 323.
24 Sheila Wingfield to Ina Boyle, 19 November 1956.
25 Sheila Wingfield to Ina Boyle, postmark 20 November 1956.
26 The other Irish composers featured in the twenty-sixth season of Radio Éireann Proms included Hamilton Harty, Gerard Victory, Carl Hardebeck, A. J. Potter and Brian Boydell.
27 Abbey Lecture Hall, 28 June 1955, broadcast Radio Éireann, 12 August 1955.
28 *Dublin Evening Mail*, 29 June 1955.
29 *Musical Times*, ci, 1408, pp. 373, 374.
30 MS TCD, 4171/8.
31 Ina Boyle to Sheila Wingfield, 18 August 1963.
32 Ina Boyle to Sheila Wingfield, 3 January 1964.
33 Ina Boyle to Sheila Wingfield, 1 June 1964.
34 Broadcast RÉ, 28 April 1964.
35 Broadcast RÉ, 4 November 1965.
36 Elizabeth Maconchy, *Ina Boyle: An Appreciation*, p. 5.
37 Monkstown Church, County Dublin, 16 March 1977, 'The Transfiguration', 'He shall swallow up death'.
38 Monkstown Church, County Dublin, 13 May 1977, *Gaelic Hymns*.
39 *Irish Times*, 17 March 1977.
40 CMC Sound Archive, RTÉ Lyric FM, CDRTÉ/26.
41 *Irish Times*, 20 October 2000.
42 Rockfinch Productions (produced by Claire Cunningham), broadcast 5 June 2010.
43 Singers include Regina Nathan, David Scott, Aylish Kerrigan, Jennifer Davis, Roger Taylor, Joan Rodgers.
44 Cathy Desmond, *Irish Examiner*, 10 September 2016.

5. A Composer's Life

1   Hugo Cole, 'Vaughan Williams Remembered', *Composer*, no. 68, Winter 1979–80, p. 26.

2   'Memoranda', p. 17.

3   *Irish Times*, 7 September 1948. According to the report, Ina's award was equivalent to second prize as there was only one other award in her section – Italy.

4   In 1952 Boyle was invited by the Art Section of the Irish Olympic Committee to send a work for consideration for the Olympics in Finland. She entered two works, subject to Edith Sitwell's permission to use her poetry. In a letter acknowledging the entry forms, dated 15 February 1952, the secretary, Máirín Allen, wrote that the titles of the works – Symphony for Contralto and Orchestra and *Still falls the rain* – 'did not imply any sports relevance', and suggested that 'a title with some hint of contest or victory or prize might help'. In the event, permission to use the poetry was refused by Sitwell.

5   Ina Boyle to Sheila Wingfield, 18 August 1963.

6   According to her mother's will (1927), Ina and Phyllis inherited the property in equal shares, apart from an annual annuity of £200 to Rev. Boyle.

7   These included the chauffeur, George Baker, his wife and five daughters; Michael Walsh, the gardener, who lived in the gate lodge with his adopted sister, May; John Moore, herdsman; and housemaids Violet Weir and Julia Garrett.

8   Sheila Wingfield, *Sun Too Fast* (London: Bles, 1974), p. 208.

9   Music by Daniel McNulty, A. J. Potter, John Reidy, Seóirse Bodley and Brian Boydell was performed.

10 Email from Nicola LeFanu, 17 December 2012.

11 MAI Papers, Manuscript Library NLI. Quartet: Anne Macnaghten, Elizabeth Rajna, Margaret Major, Arnold Ashby. 16 April 1955 Programme: Vaughan Williams, Quartet No. 2 in A minor; Purcell, *Fantasias*; Bloch, *Landscapes*; Maconchy, Quartet No. 4.

12 Sheila Wingfield to Ina Boyle, 4 April 1955.

13 Sheila Wingfield, *Sun Too Fast*, pp. 208 ff.

14 Ina Boyle to Sheila Wingfield, 12 November 1938.

15 Ina Boyle to Sheila Wingfield, 14 December 1958.

16 Ina Boyle to Sheila Wingfield, 18 August 1963.

17 *Irish Times*, 22 February 1963.

18 Ina Boyle to Sheila Wingfield, 1 June 1964.

19 Ibid.

20 TCD MS 10068, 10069. Presented to TCD Library by the BL, 19 June 1985.

21 Other women composers include Rhoda Coghill (1903–2000), Mary Dickenson-Auner (1880–1965), Adela Maddison (1863–1929), Alicia Needham (1863–1945) and Dorothy Parke (1904–1990).

22 Aloys Fleischmann (ed.), *Music in Ireland: A Symposium* (Cork: Cork University Press; Oxford: Blackwell, 1952), p. 166.

23 Ina Boyle to Sheila Wingfield, 18 August 1963.

24 Elizabeth Maconchy, *Ina Boyle: An Appreciation*, p. 3.

25 Michael Tippett, *Those Twentieth Century Blues* (London: Hutchinson, 1994), p. 15.

'The Music of Ina Boyle' (*An Essay by Séamas de Barra*)

1   Walt Whitman's poem is entitled 'Old Ireland', and is from the group of poems entitled 'Autumn Rivulets', which was added to *Leaves of Grass* in 1881 (Boston: R. Osgood & Company, 1881–82).

2   Sligo Feis Ceoil is a competitive music festival that was established in 1903 in the town of Sligo in the west of Ireland and is still held annually.

3   For an account of the conditions of musical life in Dublin and in Ireland generally during the
     second half of the nineteenth century and the first half of the twentieth century, see Jeremy
     Dibble, *Michele Esposito* (Dublin: Field Day, 2010), and Séamas de Barra, *Aloys Fleischmann*
     (Dublin: Field Day, 2006).

4   Herbert Asquith (1881–1947) was second son of H. H. Asquith, the British Prime Minister.
     He is primarily remembered now as a poet of the 1914–18 war.

5   Under its Publication Scheme, the Carnegie United Kingdom Trust published some sixty or
     so works between 1917 and 1928 when the scheme ended. Composers were invited annually
     to submit manuscript compositions in various specific classes (symphonies, concerti, operas
     and so on). These were then assessed by an anonymous board of adjudicators who chose
     up to six for publication each year. See Matthew William Erpelding, '"The danger of the
     disappearance of things": William Henry Harris' "The Hound of Heaven", unpublished
     dissertation, University of Iowa, 2014, for a brief account of the Carnegie Trust Publication
     Scheme. (Harris's *The Hound of Heaven* was one of the scores selected in 1919, the year before
     Boyle submitted *The Magic Harp*.)

6   For details of the only known performance of *Soldiers at Peace*, see p. 30.

7   In addition to *The Battle Hymn of the Republic* these are *Hymn of Heavenly Love* (Edmund
     Spenser), 1925–26; *Peace, peace! he is not dead* (Percy Bysshe Shelly), 1932; and *Hellas* (*The
     Greek Anthology*, trans. J. W. Mackail), 1941.

8   *Unseen Kings* (London: Longmans, Green & Co., 1904), pp. 63–65, 86; see also [*The
     Collected*] *Poems of Eva Gore-Booth* (London: Longmans, Green & Co., 1929), pp. 196, 205–6.

9   The misquotation appears consistently: in the MS short score, the MS full score, the MS
     orchestral parts as well as in the published score of the work. The other discrepancies relate
     to the wording, the punctuation and the capitalisation (Gore-Booth, for example, writes
     'The Wind among the Apple-trees' not 'The wind among the apple-trees').

10   See p. 6.

11   Spenser's orthography is not consistent, hence 'Colin Cloute' in *The Shepheardes Calender*
     but 'Colin Clout' elsewhere. Ina Boyle adopts the latter version and she also prefers
     'Shepheard's' to Spenser's spelling. Colin Clout seems to have been a sort of generic name
     for a youthful shepherd lad; before Spenser's time it appears in the work of John Skelton and
     after it in the work of John Gay.

12   For a description of the various stages in the composition of the symphony, see p. 20.

13   Elizabeth Maconchy, *Ina Boyle: An Appreciation, with a Select List of her Music* (Dublin: The
     Dolmen Press, 1974).

14   *In Search of Ireland* (London: Methuen & Co. Ltd., 1930), p. 41.

15   Excerpt from 'The Man Child', from the volume entitled *Irishry* published in 1913. See
     The Poems of Joseph Campbell, Austin Clarke ed. (Dublin: Allen Figgis, 1963), p. 156. After
     spending fourteen years in New York, Campbell returned to Lackandaragh in 1939, and
     lived there until his death in 1944. Campbell also found artistic inspiration in County
     Wicklow, which is reflected both in the sequence of poems that comprise *Earth of Cualann*
     (1917) and also in one of his most important later works, *A Vision of Glendalough* (published
     posthumously in 1952).

16   'The Dawn', *Earth of Cualann* (1917); see *The Poems of Joseph Campbell*, Austin Clarke ed.
     (Dublin: Allen Figgis, 1963), p. 166.

17   The most likely influence on Boyle's work is probably *A Pastoral Symphony* [No. 3] by
     Vaughan Williams, which was completed in 1921 and first performed in 1922, two
     years before the earliest version of *Glencree*. Although in four movements, *A Pastoral Symphony* is
     also predominantly meditative in character and ends with a *Lento* movement.

18   Translated by R. K. Gordon, *Anglo-Saxon Poetry* (London: J. M. Dent, 1926); this is the
     translation with which Boyle prefaces her score.

19 See p. 8.

20 The sixteen pieces that comprise the *Gaelic Hymns* include two settings of 'A Blessing', one for four-part and the other for six-part choir.

21 The two volumes published by Alexander Carmichael (1832–1912) were supplemented by four additional volumes that appeared posthumously in 1940, 1941, 1954 and 1971.

22 See pp. 24, 25.

23 The Radio Éireann Orchestra under Brian Boydell performed Scene III from *The Vision of Er* in the Phoenix Hall on 4 October 1949, and the Dublin Orchestral Players under the same conductor performed the second movement, 'Elegy', from *Virgilian Suite*, in the Metropolitan Hall, on 30 November 1950.

24 The orchestra comprises: two flutes, one oboe, cor anglais, one clarinet and one bassoon; two horns; timpani and percussion (cymbals); harp and strings.

25 The first edition of 'The Dance of Death' (1538) had forty-one woodcuts; ten further designs were added in later editions.

26 The bagpipe is cued with violin, and the tenor voice is cued with violoncello. Boyle also lists an array of 'instruments on the stage', but adds that these 'need not be played on stage, as they are imitated or played in orchestra', which suggests that they are essentially stage properties. There are also two optional speaking parts, one for Death (who speaks a Prologue and Epilogue) and another for a Minstrel (who introduces the Finale).

27 Plato, *The Republic*, trans. Benjamin Jowett (1871), ed. R. M. Hare and D. A. Russell (London: Sphere Books, 1970), p. 412. The translation of 'The Vision of Er' referred to by Boyle, and a copy of which she appended to her score, is taken from *The Republic of Plato*, tr. A. D. Lindsay (London: J. M. Dent, 1935).

28 Op. cit., p. 412.

29 Op. cit., p. 413.

30 Op. cit., p. 218.

31 Pamela Grey of Fallodon, née Wyndham (1871–1928), was the widow of Edward Tennant, First Lord Glenconnor and the second wife of distinguished British diplomat Edward Grey, First Viscount of Fallodon.

32 See Séamas de Barra, *Aloys Fleischmann* (Dublin: Field Day, 2006), pp. 43–44.

33 Alcaeus of Mytilene *c.*620–*c.*580 BC, translated by J. M. Edmonds (1875–1958), *Lyra Graeca*, vol. 1 (London: Heinemann, 1922), p. 409.

34 Benjamin Britten's Canticle III: *Still falls the rain* for tenor, horn and piano was composed in 1954.

35 The text consists of lines 85–101 and line 106 from *Of the Progress of the Soul: The Second Anniversary* (published 1612): see *John Donne: The Complete English Poems*, ed. A. J. Smith (Harmondsworth: Penguin Books, 1981), pp. 289–90.

36 Boyle's MS gives no source for the texts other than: 'From 3 Poems by Edith Sitwell (1939–1944)'.

37 *Street Songs* (London: Macmillan, 1942); *Green Song and Other Poems* (London: Macmillan, 1944). See Edith Sitwell, *Collected Poems* (London: Gerald Duckworth, 2006 [1957]), pp. 257–66.

38 Sitwell's actual line is 'Rule then the spirit working in the dark ...', but in the interest of consistency, Boyle retains the injunction 'Be', having omitted the immediately preceding lines in which the idea of ruling is introduced. Arguably, however, she also changes Sitwell's meaning, which is that Love should '*rule* the spirit', not '*be* the spirit'.

39 *The Works of Ben Jonson, with a Biographical Memoir by William Gifford* (London: Routledge, Warne & Routledge, 1860), pp. 490–501.

40 The text of the 'In summer when the shaws be sheen' [In summer when the woods are bright] consists of a somewhat modernised version of stanzas 1, 2 and 5 of *Robin Hood and the Monk* (*c.*1450).

41 One thinks, for example, of Richard Strauss's setting of Hofmansthal's *Elektra* or Vaughan Williams' setting of Synge's *Riders to the Sea*; and one of the most remarkable instances must surely be the libretto for Benjamin Britten's *A Midsummer Night's Dream* where, merely by skilfully cutting the play and rearranging the material, the composer and Peter Pears were able to retain an entirely Shakespearian text.

42 Jonson's *Dramatis Personae*, for example, contains a reference to 'Reuben, the Reconciler, a devout hermit', which gives a hint as to the direction the play might have taken, but this character makes no appearance either in the completed portion of the text or in the summary.

43 'Now sleep, and take thy rest' from Fernando de Rojas' *Celestina, or the Tragicomedy of Calisto and Melibea*, translated from the Spanish by James Mabbe (1572–1642); 'Worship, O ye that lovers be this May' is an extract (Stanza 34) in modern English from *The Kingis Quair* (The King's Book) by King James I of Scotland (1394–1437).

44 There is no actual music for these musicians, nor are the instruments they play specified in the score; they are apparently intended merely to mime their roles.

45 The chamber orchestra comprises flute, oboe, bassoon, horn, timpani, harp and string quintet (two violins, viola, violoncello and double bass).

46 The partial exceptions are Brian Boydell's Symphony for Strings of 1945 and Elizabeth Maconchy's Symphony for Double String Orchestra of 1953, which are not of course for full orchestra; and, perhaps, E. J. Moeran's Symphony in G minor of 1937, although, despite the composer's close ties with Ireland, this work properly belongs to the history of English music.

Discography

The Magic Harp Rec. Dan Godfrey Encores, Bournemouth Symphony Orchestra, conductor Ronald Corp, Dutton Epoch CD LX 7276

Wildgeese Rec. European Union Youth Orchestra, conductor Laurence Pillot, EVRO1 (2013), (Recording of Europe Day concert 11 May 2013 at Eldburg Hall, Harpa, Reykjavik, Iceland)

Three Songs by Walter de la Mare (1956); 'Sleep Song' (1923) Rec. Aylish Kerrigan (mezzo-soprano), Dearbhla Collins (piano), *I am Wind on Sea:* Contemporary Vocal Music from Ireland, Métier MSV28558 (2016)

Elegy for cello and orchestra Nadège Rochat cello and Staatskapelle Weimar, conductor Paul Meyer, CD 'Cello Abbey', Ars Produktion 2017.

Orchestral Music by Ina Boyle, BBC Concert Orchestra, Benjamin Baker violin, Nadège Rochat cello, conductor Ronald Corp, CD Dutton Epoch CDLX 7352 (2018) [containing: *A Sea Poem, Colin Clout,* Symphony No. 1, 'Glencree' (*In the Wicklow Hills*), *Psalm* for Cello and Orchestra, Concerto for Violin and Orchestra, Overture for Orchestra, *Wildgeese*].

CMC Sound Archive

9 January 1955, RÉSO, conductor Milan Horvat, RTÉ/126, *Wildgeese*

28 June 1955, RÉSO, conductor Éimear Ó Broin, RTÉ/107, *The Magic Harp*

2 January 1968, Patricia McCarry soprano, Rhoda Coghill piano, RTÉ/93 'Eternity', 'Sleep song', *Three Songs by Walter de la Mare*

17 March 1989, Ulster Orchestra, conductor Colman Pearce, CMC/63, Overture

4 February 1991, Ulster Orchestra, conductor Proinnsias Ó Duinn, CMC/63, *The Magic Harp*

13 May 1977, RTÉ Singers, conductor Eric Sweeney, RTÉ/119, three *Gaelic Hymns*

18 October 2000, National Chamber Choir, conductor Colin Mawby, CDRTÉ/26, 'O Thou! Whose Spirit'

By kind permission of TCD the following recordings have been remastered by the CMC:

TCD MS 4171/1–4 String Quartet in E minor
Macnaghten Quartet (Anne Macnaghten violin, Elise Desprez violin, Phyllis Chapman viola, Olive Richards violoncello) 10 November 1937

TCD MS 4171/5–7 *Wildgeese*
Radio Éireann Orchestra, conductor Edmond Appia, Capitol Theatre Dublin, 25 January 1948

TCD MS 4171/6 *Wildgeese*
Radio Éireann Pickup

TCD MS 4171/7
Radio Éireann Pickup
'The soul leading', Tramore Singers, conductor Stella Jacob, 27 January 1948

TCD MS 4171/8 *Still falls the rain*, contralto, string quartet, Macnaghten String Quartet (Anne Macnaghten violin, Bernard Blay violin, Pauline Jackson viola, Arnold Ashby violoncello, Margaret Cable mez sop)
Three Songs by Ben Jonson 1. 'It was a beauty that I saw', 2. 'Witch's charm' and 3. 'Flow, flow, fresh fount', for contralto, violin and violoncello (Anne Macnaghten violin, Arnold Ashby violoncello, Margaret Cable mez sop)

TCD MS 4171/9 *Thinke then, my soule*, Patrick Ring tenor, David Lillis violin, Janos Fürst violin, Máire Larchet viola, Maurice Meulien violoncello

TCD MS 4171/10 *Thinke then, my soule*
Recorded from RÉ tape

TCD MS 4171/11 *Thinke then, my soule* 4 November 1965

British Library National Sound Archive

BBC Radio 3, 4 February 1991, Ulster Orchestra, conductor Proinnsias Ó Duinn, *The Magic Harp*

BBC Radio 3, 24 October 1995 (Programme on Carnegie Publication scheme), Ulster Orchestra, conductor Proinnsias Ó Duinn, *The Magic Harp*

RTÉ Lyric FM

5 June 2010, Documentary *'From the Darkness' Ina Boyle*, Rockfinch Productions, Producer Claire Cunningham, Sonya Keogh soprano, David Brophy piano

Select Bibliography

Ashby, John and Black, Catherine (eds), 'Anne Macnaghten: Notes on a musician' (unpublished booklet, 2001)

Bowles, Michael, 'The birth of the RÉSO', *Irish Times*, 14 February 1973

Boyle, Ina, 'Songs of the Irish Gaels', *The Dominant* (OUP, February 1928)

Boyle, Dermot, *My Life, an Autobiography by Marshal of the Royal Air Force Sir Dermot Boyle G.C.B., K.C.V.O., K.B.E., A.F.C.* (published privately: 1989)

Burn, Sarah, 'Ina Boyle', *New Grove*, 4, p. 167

Campbell, Joseph, *The Poems of Joseph Campbell*, Austin Clarke ed. (Dublin: Allen Figgis, 1963)

Carmichael, Alexander, *Carmina Gadelica*, 2 vols (Edinburgh: Norman MacCleod, 1900)

Copley, Ian, *The Music of Charles Wood: A Critical Study,* 2nd edn (London: Thames Publications, 1994)

Cox, Gareth and Klein, Axel (eds), *Irish Musical Studies 7: Irish Music in the Twentieth Century* (Dublin: Four Courts Press, 2003)

Cox, Gareth, Klein, Axel and Taylor, Michael (eds), *The Life and Music of Brian Boydell* (Dublin: Irish Academic Press, 2004)

de Barra, Séamas, *Aloys Fleischmann* (Dublin: Field Day Publications, 2006)

Deale, Edgar M. (ed.), *A Catalogue of Contemporary Irish Composers* (Dublin: Music Association of Ireland, 1968; 2nd edn 1973)

Dervan, Michael (ed.), *The Invisible Art: A Century of Music in Ireland 1916–2016* (Dublin: New Island, 2016)

Dibble, Jeremy, *Michele Esposito* (Dublin: Field Day Publications, 2010)

Doctor, Jennifer, 'Working for her own Salvation', in Lewis Foreman (ed.), *Vaughan Williams in Perspective: Studies of an English Composer* (Tonbridge: Albion Music Ltd, 1998)

Edmonds, J. M., *Lyra Graeca* (London: Heinemann, 1922)

Erpelding, Matthew William, '"The danger of the disappearance of things": William Henry Harris' 'The Hound of Heaven'', unpublished dissertation (University of Iowa, 2014)

Fleischmann, Aloys (ed.), *Music in Ireland: A Symposium* (Cork: Cork University Press, 1952)

Fuller, Sophie, *The Pandora Guide to Women Composers* (London: Pandora, 1994)

Gordon, R. K., *Anglo-Saxon Poetry* (London: J. M. Dent, 1926)

Gore-Booth, Eva, *Unseen Kings* (London: Longmans Green & Co., 1904)

Heffer, Simon, *Vaughan Williams* (London: Faber & Faber, 2008)

Jephson, Maurice Denham, *An Anglo-Irish Miscellany* (Dublin: Allen Figgis, 1964)

Jonson, Ben, *The Works of Ben Jonson, with a Biographical Memoir by William Gifford* (London: Routledge, Warne & Routledge, 1860)

Keogh, Sonya, 'Ina Boyle: A Life and Work', unpublished MPhil thesis (UCC, 2002)

Leslie, Canon J. B. and Wallace, W. J. R. (eds), *Clergy of Dublin and Glendalough* (Ulster Historical Foundation and Diocesan Councils of Dublin and Glendalough, 2001)

Maconchy, Elizabeth, *Ina Boyle: An Appreciation, with a Select List of her Music* (Dublin: Dolmen Press, 1974)

McDonnell, A. H., 'Once an Inn', *Model Farming and Country Home*, December 1949

Morris, R., *The Works of Edmund Spenser* (London: Macmillan & Co., 1893)

Morton, H. V., *In Search of Ireland* (London: Methuen & Co., 1930)

Ó Broin, Éimear, 'Music and Broadcasting', in Richard Pine (ed.), *Music in Ireland 1848–1998, Thomas Davis Lectures* (Cork: Mercier Press, 1998)

O'Kelly, Pat, *The National Symphony Orchestra of Ireland 1948–1998: A Selected History* (Dublin: RTÉ, 1998)

Perrick, Penny, *Secrets to Hide: The Life of Sheila Wingfield, Viscountess Powerscourt* (Dublin: The Lilliput Press, 2007)

Pine, Richard, *Music and Broadcasting in Ireland* (Dublin: Four Courts Press, 2005)

Plato, *The Republic*, trans. Benjamin Jowett (1871), R. M. Hare and D. A. Russell (eds) (London: Sphere Books, 1970)

Probert, Henry A., 'Boyle, Sir Dermot Alexander (1904–1993)', *Oxford Dictionary of National Biography* (Oxford: OUP, 2004)

Scholes, Percy, *New Works by Modern British Composers*, second series, Carnegie UK Trust Publication Scheme (London: Stainer & Bell, 1924)

Sitwell, Edith, *Collected Poems* (London: Gerald Duckworth, 2006)

Smith, A. J. (ed.), *John Donne: The Complete English Poems* (Harmondsworth: Penguin Books, 1981)

Walsh, Basil, *Michael W. Balfe* (Dublin: Irish Academic Press, 2008)

White, Brian, *The Little Book of Bray and Enniskerry* (Dublin: The History Press Ireland, 2016)

Wingfield, Sheila, 'Powerscourt and Ina Boyle', in Sheila Wingfield, *Sun Too Fast* (London: Bles, 1974)

Conference Papers: Ita Beausang (2009–2016)

2009   RIAM SMI/RMA Joint Annual Conference, 'Connections and disconnections: Ina Boyle and music in Dublin 1939–1955'

2010	University of Durham Music Department Conference on Irish Music and Musicians, 'Sudden fame for Irish woman composer'
2011	RIAM SMI Conference, 'Nature versus nurture: Conflicting elements in the life and music of Ina Boyle'
2012	RIAM Women and Music in Ireland Conference, 'Lady with cello: Three compositions by Ina Boyle'
2013	DIT Symposium, 'The Development of the Symphony in Ireland', 'From Glencree to Amalfi: Ina Boyle's symphonic journey'
2014	St Patrick's College Drumcondra, Women and Music in Ireland Conference, 'a kind of children's opera ... *Maudlin of Paplewick* by Ina Boyle'
2014	TCD Long Room Hub, 'In Tune: A Millenium of Music in TCD Library', 'No coward soul is mine: Ina Boyle's legacy'
2016	DIT Conservatory of Music and Drama, 'Music in Ireland: 1916 and Beyond', 'Ina Boyle's parallel narrative'

Articles online

| 2012 | 'An Irish composer and the 1948 Olympics', journalofmusic.com/focus/olympic-talent |
| 2014 | 'An Irish composer and World War I', www.enniskerryhistory.org/home |

Websites

www.inaboyle.org
Contemporary Music Centre: http://www.cmc.ie
Ina Boyle Facebook Page: https://www.facebook.com/InaBoyle/
Michael Jamieson Bristow: http://www.michaeljamiesonbristow.ina-boyle-1889-1967
Sonya Keogh: http://www.sonyakeogh.com
http://www.kcl/iss/library/spec/collections/indiv/carnegie.html
TCD Digital Collections, http:digitalcollections.tcd.ie/home: digital copies of a selection of Ina Boyle's manuscripts and note-books

Index